CONTROLLING RESTAURANT & FOOD SERVICE
FOOD COSTS

By Douglas R. Brown

The Food Service Professional's Guide To:
Controlling Restaurant & Food Service Food
Costs: 365 Secrets Revealed

Atlantic Publishing Group, Inc. Copyright © 2003
1210 SW 23rd Place
Ocala, Florida 34474
800-541-1336
352-622-5836 - Fax

www.atlantic-pub.com - Web site
sales@atlantic-pub.com - E-mail

SAN Number :268-1250

International Standard Book Number: 0-910627-16-9

Library of Congress Cataloging-in-Publication Data

Brown, Douglas Robert, 1960-
Controlling restaurant & food service food costs : 365 secrets
revealed / by Douglas R. Brown.
p. cm. -- (Food service professionals guide to ; 6)
Includes bibliographical references and index.
ISBN 0-910627-16-9 (pbk. : alk. paper)
1. Food service--Cost control. 2. Food prices. I. Title:
Controlling restaurant and food service food costs. II. Title.
III. Series.
TX911.3.C65 B74 2003
647.95'068'1--dc21
2002013540

Printed in Canada

Book layout and design by Meg Buchner of Megadesign
www.mega-designs.com • e-mail: megadesn@mhtc.net

CONTENTS

INTRODUCTION

If you operate a food service organization, you have to buy food products; that's the reality. The largest expenditure for most food service organizations is the cost of food. However, in this book we will show you many ways to reduce your food costs. Even a 3 percent reduction in food costs for a restaurant grossing $1,000,000 with food costs of $400,000 means an approximate savings of $12,000, which will go straight to your bottom line.

In order to control food costs effectively, there are four essential things that you need to do:
1. Forecast how much and what you are going to sell.
2. Purchase, receive and prepare according to these forecasts.
3. Portion effectively.
4. Control money, waste and theft.

Thankfully, improvements in technology and management techniques allow smart restaurant operators to keep food costs within the boundaries needed to generate a profit, while still providing their customers with the level of service that they need to generate repeat business. A restaurant manager must be prepared to develop and monitor cost-control programs, particularly food cost, to maintain profitability.

Unless you make changes, this book is of no use to you. You must begin to change your thinking and your methods. Take them one at a time, and make them a part of your business. Many of these tips will not only cut your food costs, but will also enhance your finished products. Better food brings more business, which brings more money. A reduction in your food costs means that you can keep more of that money. Armed with the information in this book, you will find actual tips that produce profitable results, without consuming all your time in unnecessary research or worse: experiences of painful trial, risk and error.

CHAPTER ONE

OVERVIEW

The Basics

Controlling food cost is basically about two concepts: First, ensuring that all food and revenue is accounted for and utilized in the most efficient manner. Second, ensuring that every ounce of food purchased is sold at the maximum allowable price. The following sections will present a system of cost controls. Combining these controls with basic procedures and policies as outlined in this book will enable you to establish an airtight food cost-control system.

Getting Organized

Organization is the easiest and cheapest manner of generating productivity and reducing food costs. The mere act of putting instructions on paper or giving your staff a checklist, instead of having to hold their hand through a process, can save your company thousands.

- **Organizational and structure component charts.** Use organizational charts to know and understand who does what in your restaurant on a daily, weekly and monthly basis. How can this structure improve? Are jobs allocated in the most productive manner possible? Written job descriptions are good tools to use for this. You can find examples of job descriptions and a questionnaire for writing job descriptions at www.hrnext.com. Atlantic Publishing offers a complete set of restaurant job descriptions on computer disk at www.atlantic-pub.com.

- **Use checklists for yourself.** Create a checklist of items you perform every day and organize your time. Of course, variations from this checklist will always occur, but you will cover the basics a lot faster with a guide in hand. This will save you and your staff time and confusion.

- **Where to find forms and checklists.** This book utilizes forms and checklists for cost-control procedures. You can certainly create your own forms based on the templates provided in this book using a computer or manual system. However, all of these forms and many more (over 80 total) are available on CD-ROM with the purchase of *The Restaurant Manager's Handbook* (3rd Edition) by calling 800-541-1336 or visiting www.atlantic-pub.com (Item RMH-02).

Food Sales and Costs Survey

Before you can determine the best ways to reduce your food cost, you to need look at your sales and cost figures. Take a look at the following food sales and costs statistics. How does your operation compare?

THE 2002 RESTAURANT FOOD SALES & COSTS SURVEY

Type of Restaurant	Food Sales	Cost of Food
Full-service	70-75%	26-40%
Fast-service	90-95%	25-35%

What Does Your Food-Cost Percentage Really Mean?

Johnny's steak house has a food cost of 38 percent; Sally's steak house has a food cost of 44 percent. Which is a more efficient operator? Which is more profitable? Your restaurant has a food cost in January of 38 percent; in February it is 32 percent. Did you operate more efficiently the second month? The answer to these questions is: we just don't know. There is not enough information to determine this from the figures; we need to know what the food-cost percentage should have been as well.

- **Importance of food-cost percentages.** Don't become overly concerned over food cost percentages, they are truly meaningless unless you know what your food-cost percentage should be for the given time in question. Remember, you get paid in and deposit dollars into the bank, not percentages.

- **Weighted food-cost percentage.** Once your food cost is calculated, you must determine your weighted food-cost percentage. A weighted food cost percentage will tell you what your food cost should have been over a given period of time if all procedures and controls in place operated at 100-percent efficiency. We will show you how to determine a weighted food cost in a later section.

Food Cost-Control Records - Get it Right

In order to control food costs, you must first know what your costs are. Accurate record keeping is essential in implementing a cost-control system.

- **Controlling large operations.** The larger the distance between an owner or manager and the actual restaurant, the greater the need for effective cost-control records. This is how franchisers of restaurant chains keep their eyes on thousands of units across the world.

- **Give managers information.** Many managers of individual operations assume that since they're on the premises during operating hours, a detailed system of cost control is unnecessary. Tiny family operations often see controls the same way and view any device for theft prevention as a sign of distrust towards their staff. This is shortsighted because the main purpose of cost control is to provide information to management about daily operations.

- **Theft prevention.** Prevention of theft is a secondary function. Cost controls are about knowing where you are going. Furthermore, most waste and inefficiencies cannot be seen; they need to be understood through the numbers.

- **Definitions.** You must be able to understand the numbers related to food cost and be able to interpret them. To do this effectively, you need to understand the difference between control and reduction:
  1. *Control* is achieved through the assembly and interpretation of data and ratios on your revenue and expenses.

  2. *Reduction* is the actual action taken to bring costs within your predetermined standards. Effective cost control starts at the top of an organization. Management must establish, support and enforce its standards and procedures.

Get Computerized

No matter what type or size of food service operation you run, our advice is to get your operation computerized. It's extremely difficult to compete successfully without utilizing technology, at least to some degree. Today the investment for a basic computer and accounting software is less than $2,000 and could be as little as $1,000. The investment will deliver immediate savings in accounting fees and your ability to get true insight into your business.

- **QuickBooks.** Our favorite restaurant accounting package, based on price and ease of use, is the veteran QuickBooks® by Intuit. The 2002 version of QuickBooks® is rich in features including built-in remote-access capabilities and Web interfaces. Reports that would take hours to calculate manually are generated in a few seconds. The reports are also flawless, eliminating the human-error factor. This program now has a POS option that was the only limiting factor in previous releases. QuickBooks® is available at www.quickbooks.com. Another popular accounting package is Peachtree®, available at www.peachtree.com.

- **Tasty Profits software.** If you are just setting up your accounting program and decide to use QuickBooks®, we recommend an add-on product called The Tasty Profits Guide to QuickBooks® Software for Restaurants. This helpful guide to QuickBooks® enables you to save thousands of dollars doing your own accounting with its proven, easy-to-use system. Simply install the floppy disc that is included with the "Tasty Profits Guide" directly into your computer. After downloading the pre-configured restaurant accounts, you'll be ready to go. You will have instant access to all your financial data. You will also be able to calculate accurate food and bar costs, reconcile bank and credit card statements, track and pay tips that are charged to credit cards, and calculate sales tax automatically. The program costs about $70 and is available at www.atlantic-pub.com, 800-541-1336 (Item TP-01).

- **Utilize the same chart of accounts to compare your operation with others.** Ratios enable you to compare the operating data of a specific hotel or restaurant to the average for a group of similar establishments. You may, for example, compare the food cost and food sales of a particular restaurant with the average sales and costs of restaurants of a similar size.

- **Operations report.** The National Restaurant Association publishes a report entitled "The Operations Report," an annual survey based on operator income statements that is conducted jointly by the association and the accounting firm of Deloitte & Touche. The report provides detailed data on where the restaurant dollar comes from and where it goes for four categories of restaurants: three types of full-service operations (with per-person check sizes under $10; between $10 and $25; and $25 and more) and limited-service operations (fast food). You can use this report to compare your operation to others.

- **Four-week accounting period.** Companies typically close their books and prepare financial statements at the end of each month. The problem for retail businesses such as restaurants is that there are uneven numbers of days and uneven numbers of the type of days in a month. For example, you may have an extra Saturday in a month which would skew sales numbers upwards. Consider using a four-week accounting period so you can compare apples to apples.

- **POS (point-of-sale) systems are crucial for reducing loss.** The most widely used technology in the food service industry is the touch-screen. The POS system is basically an offshoot of the electronic cash register. Touch-screen POS systems were introduced to the food service industry in the mid-1980s and have penetrated 90 percent of restaurants nationwide. (See Chapter 9 for more information on POS systems.)

The Key to Controlling Food Cost is Reconciliation

The key to controlling food cost is reconciliation. Every step or action in the cost-control process is checked and reconciled with another person. Once these systems are set up, management's responsibility is to monitor them with daily involvement. Should all the steps and procedures be adhered to, you will know exactly where every dollar and ounce of food went; there are no loopholes.

- **Teach them.** Management must be involved in the training and supervision of all employees. For any cost-control system to work, employees must be trained and know what actions are expected of them. It is management's responsibility to supervise employees and see that they receive this training.

- **Communicate.** Daily involvement and communication is needed in order to succeed. Employees must follow all procedures precisely. If they do not, they must be informed of their specific deviations from these procedures and correct them. This is a daily task that involves a hands-on management style.

- **Enforce.** Any control initiated is only as good as the manager who follows up and enforces it. The total amount of time a manager needs to complete all of the work that will be described in this section is less than one hour a day. There is no excuse for not completing each procedure every day. A deviation in your controls or involvement can only lead to a loss over the control of the restaurant's costs.

- **Tracking.** Although a simple manual system is detailed here, many of your cost-control procedures can be tracked through your computerized accounting system and/or POS system. Many of the basic purchasing and receiving functions are found in virtually all off-the-shelf accounting programs.

Practical Examples

Finally, the kitchen controls section combines all the personnel and procedures previously described into a system of checks and balances. This section will enable the restaurant manager, through the use of the sample forms and simple procedures, to know exactly where every food item and every cent the restaurant business spent.

To enable you to envision precisely how the personnel procedures and controls combine to control the restaurant's food cost, a summary of the key points are listed in this section in sequence of events.

In the example, you will trace 25 pounds of shrimp through a typical day's operation, from the initial purchase to reconciling the revenue. The first column in each of the example forms are filled out so you will be able to see how they are used and why each one is a critical part in the overall control system. We would recommend that the manager put the following list in the form of a check-off sheet for his or her own organizational purposes.

Sample sequence of events:

1. Determine the need to purchase shrimp.

2. Purchase the amount needed. Example: 25 pounds.

3. Shrimp is delivered. Follow the receiving and storing procedures.

4. Enter the amount delivered on the Perpetual Inventory Form. Example: 5 boxes of 5 pounds each.

ITEM		1	2	3	4	5	6	7	8	9	10	11	12	13	14	15	16	17	18	19	20	21	22	23	24	25	26	27	28	29	30	31	1
Shrimp (20)	+ 5																																
(5 lbs.)	- 1																																
	= 24																																

5. Preparation cooks compute the opening counts from the previous evening. Example: 25 shrimp dinners is the beginning count.

ITEM	MINIMUM AMOUNT	AMOUNT DEF./ORD.	BEGINNING AMOUNT	AMOUNT PREPPED	STARTING TOTAL
Shrimp	33	5 lbs.	25	9	34

6. The minimum amount needed as determined by sale history is 33. The preparation cooks need to prepare 9 more dinners for that night.

7. Cooks remove 5 pounds, or 1 box, of shrimp from the freezer.

8. Cooks sign out the 5 pounds of shrimp on the Sign-out Sheet.

ITEM	DATE	AMOUNT/WT.	EMPLOYEE
Shrimp-box	11-30	1-5lb. box	Joe B.

9. The amount, 5 pounds, is placed in the "Amount Defrosted or Ordered" column on the Preparation Sheet.

ITEM	MINIMUM AMOUNT	AMOUNT DEF./ORD.	BEGINNING AMOUNT	AMOUNT PREPPED	STARTING TOTAL
Shrimp	33	(5 lbs.)	25	9	34

10. The shrimp is prepared as prescribed in the Recipe and Procedure Manual.

11. The cooks prepare nine 8.5-ounce dinners; enter this figure in the amount prepared column. The starting total would be 9 + 25 = 34. Enter these figures on the Preparation Form.

ITEM	MINIMUM AMOUNT	AMOUNT DEF./ORD.	BEGINNING AMOUNT	AMOUNT PREPPED	STARTING TOTAL
Shrimp	33	5 lbs.	25	9	34

12. The Preparation Form is completed and given to the kitchen director or manager. All storage areas are locked before leaving.

13. The invoices are brought to the manager's office.

14. The kitchen director computes the yields.

ITEM	STARTING WEIGHT (OZ.)	# OF PORTIONS	TOTAL PORTION WEIGHT (OZ.)	YIELD %	PREP. COOK
Shrimp dinner	80.0	9	9 x 8.0oz = 72 oz.	90%	Bob S.

15. The cooks come in for the evening and count all the items for the Starting Total.

ITEM	START	ADDITIONS	STARTING BALANCE	BALANCE ENDING	# SOLD
Shrimp dinners	*25*	*9*	*34*	*21*	*13*

16. The manager verifies that the Starting Total on the Preparation Form is the same as on the Cook's Form.

17. The manager issues the tickets to the waitstaff. The manager issues the cashier drawer to the cashier and verifies the starting amount.

WAITPERSON	TOT #	#THRU	INITIALS	RETURN # VERIFIED

18. The manager checks the perpetual inventory (the daily usage of your main entrée items).

19. The waitstaff gives the order tickets to the kitchen expediter.

20. The expediter reads off the items to the cooks who start to cook the menu items.

21. When completed, the waiter/waitress takes the dinner to the customer.

22. The bill is totaled and given to the customer.

23. The cashier verifies the amount and collects the money or charge.

24. The cooks count the balance ending. Example: Starting total is 34; ending balance is 21; 13 were sold.

ITEM	START	ADDITIONS	STARTING BALANCE	BALANCE ENDING	# SOLD
Shrimp dinners	25	9	34	21	13

25. The expediter itemizes the carbon copies. Thirteen shrimp dinners were sold.

26. The manager cashes out with the cashier. Ticket itemization shows 13 shrimp dinners sold.

ITEM	USE A ✔ MARK TO DESIGNATE ONE SOLD	TOTAL SOLD
Shrimp dinner	✓✓✓✓✓✓✓✓✓✓✓✓✓	13

27. All three figures are verified: cooks to expediter to cashier.

28. The following morning the manager verifies the ending balance of the cook's form (21) to the beginning count of the preparation form.

ITEM	START	ADDITIONS	STARTING BALANCE	BALANCE ENDING	# SOLD
Shrimp dinners	25	9	34	21	13

29. The bookkeeper rechecks and verifies all the transactions of the previous night, ensuring that 13 shrimp dinners were sold and the money was accounted for.

75 POSSIBLE FOOD-COST PROBLEM AREAS

1. No balance of high- and low-cost items on the menu.

2. No consideration of locally obtainable products.

3. No competitive purchasing plan.

4. Theft in any form.

5. Purchasing more than needed (spoilage).

6. No daily check of invoices, quality and prices.

7. Improper rotation procedures.

8. Too many items on the menu.

9. Not enough low price - high food-cost percentage items on the menu.

10. No perpetual inventory in place.

11. No controls on issuing items from storage areas.

12. Low yields on products.

13. Over-preparing (waste, spoilage).

14. Approving invoices without checking deliveries and following procedures.

15. Not using or following exact standardized recipes.

16. Not following exact portion sizes.

17. Improper handling (wrapping, rotating, storing).

18. No reconciliation of food sold vs. food consumed.

19. Employee pilferage including snacking on food items.

20. Orders not correctly received.

21. Frozen food not rotated.

22. Negative relationships with suppliers.

23. Freezer doors not closed properly.

24. Dry foods not stored properly allowing spoilage and bug infestation.

25. Not implementing a HACCP program.

26. Freezers and walk-ins located too close to back door, convenient for theft.

27. The manager not occasionally checking the dumpster and garbage cans at an unexpected time.

28. Use clear plastic containers in the kitchen to collect "waste." Each kitchen staffer should get his or her own container. Garbage cans are too easy to throw "waste" into.

29. Credit not received from vendor for returned merchandise.

30. Chemicals stored next to food causing possible poisoning.

31. Dry food areas are not well organized causing over-ordering.

32. Frozen-food area is not well organized causing over-ordering.

33. Perishable items left out of refrigerated area.

34. Food used in the bar and recorded in bar sales.

35. Failure to raise prices when food costs increase.

36. Food purchased at cost for personal use.

37. No reconciling of kitchen checks and guest checks.

38. Hors d'oeuvres that were given free to bar patrons.

39. No guest check rung up for house, complimentary or manager food.

40. Over-consumption – not portioning salad dressings.

41. Opened containers not properly sealed developing spoilage because of air flow.

42. Frozen products stored too close together.

43. Rusty and/or dirty shelving.

44. Supply room doors not locked.

45. Reprocessing of previously paid invoices for payment.

46. Poor paperwork and use of control forms.

47. Poorly trained employees.

48. Cooking equipment temperatures not regularly calibrated.

49. Scales not regularly calibrated or replaced.

50. Over-production.

51. The staff deliberately creating mistakes so they can consume them.

52. Burned or overcooked food due to poor training.

53. Not weighing portions.

54. Cold food being returned by customers.

55. Incorrect garnishing procedures.

56. Incorrect addition or totaling on guest checks.

57. Not portioning margarine and butter.

58. Food being discounted or not reordered on a ticket.

59. Not removing all contents from cans and bottles.

60. Resetting or "Z"-ing cash register readings.

61. Spoilage due to incorrect thawing procedures.

62. Equipment used in food preparation not scraped of excess food prior to washing.

63. Not using standardized recipes.

64. Discarding unopened food containers which could be recycled.

65. Not charging for coffee, tea, sodas, etc.

66. NSF checks and invalid credit cards being accepted.

67. Brewing too much coffee, ice tea or tea.

68. Prepared food dropped on the floor.

69. Failure to take discounts offered for early payment from vendors.

70. No control system in place for guest tickets.

71. No control of after-dinner mints.

72. Servers receiving food from kitchen without recording sales.

73. Dull knives.

74. Fake company invoices being sent for payment.

75. Rotation and color-coded, day-dated labels not used.

CHAPTER TWO

MATH AND COST RATIOS

The Beginning Inventory

Owners and managers need to be on the same page in terms of the meaning and calculation of the many ratios used to analyze food costs. It's important to understand how your ratios are being calculated so you can get a true indication of the cost or profit activity in your restaurant. Cost control is not just the calculation of these numbers; it's the interpretation of them and the appropriate (re)actions taken to bring your numbers within set standards.

- **Beginning Inventory.** The beginning inventory is the total dollar value of food supplies on hand at the beginning of the accounting period. This figure represents the starting point from which you can then compute total food cost each month.

- **Computing the beginning inventory** is a simple calculation. If you are purchasing all new food products, simply total all your food purchases prior to opening day. This figure will be the beginning inventory.

- **Opening an old restaurant at a new location.** If you are opening an existing restaurant and will be using some of the old supplies, first take an inventory of the old supplies. Add the dollar value of these supplies with all your new food purchases prior to opening day.

The Ending Inventory

An ending inventory is taken for a complete and accurate count of the food stock on hand at the end of an accounting period so that the remaining amount may be used in projecting the total cost for each category. When conducting the ending or physical inventory:

- **Use scales.** For the most accurate determination, use scales.

- **Stocking order.** Place inventory sheets in the same order as the room is stocked.

- **Separate sheets.** Use a separate sheet for each area.

- **Include the following on the form:** your inventory unit, units per case, pack or size, par and vendor code.

- **Use two people:** one to count (a manager) and one to record the figures (preferably an employee from a different area). For example, have the bar manager assist in the food inventory. One will count while the other writes. The person counting states each item, its unit and its total amount. The other employee enters the figure on the inventory sheet on the correct line.

- **Partial items.** If there is a partial item, such as half a case of tomatoes, estimate how much on a scale from 0.1 to 0.9 (0.5 being half of a container). Make sure there is a figure on either side of the decimal point (e.g., 0.5, 1.3).

- **Counting order.** Count shelves all the way across. Do not jump around.

- **Fill in all columns.** Put a zero (0) in columns where there is no item to be counted.

- **Use pound and unit costs.** Convert all items that are in prepared form into pound and unit costs. For example: 15 fish dinners at 12.5 oz = 11.72 lbs.

- **Multiples.** For multiple weights or numbers of items, use a separate pad and double check the entries.

- **Double-check.** Make sure there's an entry for each item.

- **Be thorough.** Complete each area before moving on to a new one and check for blanks and possible mistakes.

- **Estimating.** When estimates must be made, they should be made with sound reasoning, not guessing.

Food-Cost Percentage

Food Cost of Sales Calculation	
Beginning inventory +	$5,000.00
Purchases +	$100,000.00
Total =	$105,000.00
Ending Inventory −	$35,000.00
Food used =	$70,000.00
*Employee meals, comp. food, manager −	$3,000.00
Cost of Food Sold	**$67,000.00**
Divide the Cost of Food Sold by the Food Sales	
Food Sales	**$175,000.00**
Food-Cost Percentage	**38.29%**

This basic ratio is often misinterpreted because it is calculated in so many different ways. Basically, it is food cost divided by food sales. Whether your food cost is determined by food sold or consumed is a crucial difference. For your food-cost percentage to be accurate, a month-end inventory must be taken. Without this figure, your food-cost statement is inaccurate and, therefore, basically useless because your inventory will vary month to month, even in the most stable environment.

Employee meals, complimentary food and manager-consumed food are removed from the food-cost equation as these costs should be reclassified on the P&L. Employee meals are an employee benefit; complimentary meals are considered promotional costs; and manager meals are a management benefit.

- **Distinguishing between food sold and consumed is important.** Food consumed includes all food used, sold, wasted, stolen or given away to customers and employees. Food sold is determined by subtracting all food bought (at full price) from the total food consumed. (See the example above.)

Cost Calculations - The Basics

Maximum allowable food-cost percentage (MFC). This is the most food can cost for you to meet your profit goal. If your food-cost percentage is over your maximum allowable percentage at the end of the month, you won't meet your profit expectations. This is how you calculate it:

1. Write your dollar amounts of labor costs and overhead expenses (exclude food costs). Refer to past accounting periods and yearly averages to get realistic cost estimates.

2. Add your monthly profit goal as either a dollar amount or a percentage of sales.

3. Convert dollar values of expenses to percentages by dividing by food sales for the periods used for expenses. Generally, don't use your highest or

lowest sales figures for calculating your operating expenses. Subtract the total of the percentages from 100 percent. The remainder is your maximum allowable food-cost percentage (MFC).

4. 100 – (monthly expenses – food costs) + monthly profit goal = %MFC

- **Actual food-cost percentage (AFC).** This is the percentage at which you're actually operating. It's calculated by dividing food cost by food sales (only food sales, not total sales). If you are deducting employee meals from your income statement, then you are calculating cost of food sold. If there is no deduction of employee meals, which is true for most operations, then the food cost you're reading is food consumed. This is always a higher cost than food sold. If inventory is not being taken, the food cost on your income statement is just an estimate based on purchases and isn't accurate.

- **Potential food-cost percentage (PFC).** This cost is sometimes called the theoretical food cost. PFC is the lowest your food cost can be because it assumes that all food consumed is sold and that there is no waste whatsoever. Calculate this cost by multiplying the number sold of each menu item by the ideal recipe cost.

- **Standard food cost (SFC).** This is how you adjust for the unrealistically low PFC. The percentage includes unavoidable waste, employee meals, etc. This food-cost percentage is compared to the AFC and is the standard that management must meet.

- **The prime cost includes the cost of direct labor with food cost.** This cost includes labor incurred because the item is made from scratch (labor from baking pies and bread, trimming steaks, etc.). When the food cost is determined for these items, the cost of the labor needed to prepare them is added. This costing method is applied to every menu item needing extensive direct labor before it is served to the customer. Indirect labor cannot be attributed to any particular menu item and is overhead.

- **Beverage exclusions.** Beverage sales should not include coffee, tea, milk or juice, which are usually considered food. If you include soft drinks in your food costs, be aware that it will reduce the food cost, since the ratio of cost to selling price is so low.

- **Ratio of food to beverage sales.** This is simply the ratio of the percentages of your total sales. In restaurants with a higher percentage of beverage than food sales, profits are generally higher because there is a greater profit margin on beverages.

- **Sales mix.** Sales mix is the number of each menu item sold. It's crucial to cost analysis because each item impacts food cost and food percentages differently.

Weighted Food-Cost Percentage

Once your food cost is calculated, determine weighted food-cost percentage. A weighted food cost percentage will tell you what your food cost should have been had all procedures and controls operated at 100-percent efficiency. The following schedule summarizes sales information from the restaurant's POS system, or from other bookkeeping records. Basically, you are recreating the food cost for each item based on the standard recipe costs to determine what your food cost and, thus, food-cost percentage should have been. For this example we will pretend that only four menu items are served in this restaurant. From this example you can see that $7,000 of food costs have slipped away (assuming all calculations are accurate). The restaurant should have actually had a 34.28 percent weighted food cost percentage.

WEIGHTED FOOD-COST CHART

Menu Item	Cost per Meal	#. of Meals Served	Cost per Menu Item
Chicken Kiev	$5.00	2,000	$10,000.00
Steak Oscar	$8.00	4,000	$32,000.00
Stuffed Flounder	$9.00	1,000	$9,000.00
Hamburger Platter	$3.00	3,000	$9,000.00

Weighted Total Cost	**$60,000.00**
Actual Sales	$175,000.00
Weighted Food-Cost Percentage	34.28%
Variation Over Actual Food-Cost Percentage	4% or $7,000.00

Daily Food-Cost Analysis

Traditionally, food cost is calculated once a month. There is no reason, however, why you cannot compute a daily food cost and a daily weighted food cost to analyze problem areas. Much of the inventory counting can be eliminated by moving only the products used for production into the kitchen at the beginning of the shift. In this way, you can pinpoint problem areas, problem employees or problem shifts. You can also calculate a separate food cost for breakfast or lunch.

Raising Prices

Want to immediately lower your food-cost percentage? Raise your prices. At some point in your career as a food service manager, you have to deal with the issue of raising prices.

- **Reasons for raising prices.** Make an overall review of your establishment. You may be experiencing higher food costs because food prices have risen significantly since your last price review. Perhaps you have just undergone major renovation and have upgraded the atmosphere of your restaurant. Competition may have changed since the last increase, or you may have decided that you need to make a bigger profit in order for it to be worthwhile to stay in business. All of these are valid reasons for price increases. The way to implement increases, however, should be considered carefully.

- **Target certain items first.** If you do an across-the-board price increase, you may scare off some customers. You may want to consider increasing the price on a certain number of key dishes and leaving other price increases for a later date.

- **Decide how to communicate these increases.** Should you print a new menu or devise a way to increase the price on existing copies of the menu? It's never a good idea to simply cross out the old price and write in the new. But, many food service managers also feel that it is a bad idea to increase prices when you print new menus that have changes in the items being offered. Whatever you decide, don't alert customers to price increases!

- **Test market?** It may be best to reprint old menus with new prices and save any changes to the bill of fare until a later printing. This strategy will also let you "test market" the new prices. If you're not seeing the sales you need from the new prices, you can adjust them with a second printing.

CHAPTER THREE

THE MENU, PRICING & STANDARDIZED RECIPES

Menu Sales

The menu is where you begin to control food costs. Consider the following basic requirements:

- **Functionality.** Once your concept is decided, your equipment and kitchen space requirements should be designed around the recipes on your menu. Once a kitchen has been built, there is, of course, some flexibility to menu changes, but new pieces of equipment may be impossible to add without high costs or renovations. To design correctly, you need to visualize delivery, processing, preparation, presentation and washing. To do this, you must be intimately familiar with each menu item.

Pricing

Pricing is an important aspect of your revenues and customer counts. Prices that are too high will drive customers away and prices that are too low will kill your profits. Pricing is not the simple matter of appropriate markup over cost, it combines other factors as well. Prices can be either market driven or demand driven.

- **Market-driven items.** Market-driven prices must be responsive to your competitors' prices. Common dishes that both you and the place down the road sell need to be priced competitively. This is also true when you're introducing new items for which a demand has not been developed.

- **Demand-driven items.** These are items which customers ask for and where demand exceeds your supply. You have a short-term monopoly on these items and, therefore, price is driven up until demand slows or competitors begin to sell similar items.

- **Markup.** A combination of methods is usually a good idea, since each menu item is usually different. Two basic theories are: charge as much as you can, and charge as little as you can. Each has its pluses and minuses. Obviously, if you charge as much as you can, you increase the chance of greater profits. You do, however, run the risk of needing to offer a product those customers feel is worth the price, otherwise you will lose them because they won't think you're a good value. Charging the lowest price you can gives customers a great sense of value but lowers your profit margin per item.

Food-Cost Tracking

Cost is the basic building block of menu pricing, so you need to understand how to track food cost in order to price your menu for maximum profits. Before you price your menu, you need to cost out each menu item. This information can come from your standardized recipe, or you can create a separate cost sheet that lists all the items on the menu.

- **Costs should be based on a standardized recipe.** Consistency in operations, costs and customer expectations are why all recipes must be standardized. Take the example of a little restaurant chain called McDonald's. What do they do best? They serve consistent, hot food fast, whether you order the Big Mac™ hamburger in London, Tokyo or Chicago. When you order, you know exactly what you are going to receive. You want your customers to know what they are going to receive each and every time.

- **Standardized recipes.** What would be your reaction if you went to a favorite restaurant for their huge prime rib and you received a much smaller portion than usual? Marketing surveys indicate that 60-90 percent of the revenue of independent restaurants is generated from return business. Standardized recipes are the only way you can have accurate costs and a viable business. Think of your business as a manufacturing plant. Every toaster that GE produces is identical regardless of the employee assembling the unit. You need a standard recipe for every item you prepare: bread, salad dressings, sauces, garnishes, side dishes, etc.

Here are some of the advantages of using standardized recipes:

- Customers will communicate to others about your great food, generous portions and terrific service.

- It ensures product consistency, uniform quality and taste.

- The waitstaff will know what dish they will receive and can communicate to the customer what to expect.

- The customer will know what to expect.

- It improves cost control by controlling portion size.

- It lists item's costs, which makes it easy to access and use this information for pricing.

- It helps make the kitchen run smoother and more efficiently.

- It helps create inventory and purchasing lists.

- It helps with employee training.

- Less supervision is needed during preparation.

- You will need less highly trained (highly paid) staff.

- You will have better food-cost control.

- It will be possible to calculate the cost of each meal accurately.

- **Menu item cost information.** Bear in mind that while the standardized recipe is an obvious place to list menu item costs, it may not be the only place. More than likely, you and your kitchen staff aren't keeping current with cost changes. Try keeping menu item cost information on a separate sheet with your invoices and other purchasing paperwork. This way you can easily monitor your food costs and keep track of any changes.

- **Laminate your standard recipe cards** and place them in several locations in the kitchen. Use a Polaroid or digital camera to record how the finished dish should look including the correct plate and garnish to use. Place this photo on the recipe card.

- **Chefs and experienced line cooks may be resistant to following standard recipes.** In your restaurant you can only have one way to prepare each menu item.

Consider the following when developing your recipe file:

- Test all recipes in your kitchen.

- Have ingredients listed in the order they are used.

- Check for correct ingredient amounts.

- Make sure the sequence of activities is clear.

- Make sure you have all the necessary equipment to prepare the recipe. If your staff is using various pans to cook something because you don't have the correct size, the item will not turn out the same each time and you are forfeiting consistency.

- Give dry ingredients measure by weight and liquid ingredients by volume. Be sure you have a scale to measure the weighed amounts.

- Make sure that you or a designated person records any changes to the recipe over time.

- Use it! Make sure you enforce the use of standard-ized recipes with your kitchen staff.

- List the appropriate plate and garnish and, if at all possible, include a photo.

- **Recipe holders.** Use index cards and an index cardholder to hold your recipes. Alternatively, use a three-ring binder with recipe sheets inserted into transparent envelopes that can be easily wiped clean.

- **Organize your file in a meaningful way.** Group all the appetizers together, all the soups, all the entrées, all the salads and all the desserts.

Recipe Information

Although your recipe file will change over time, it should always contain certain basic pieces of information. Make sure that you keep track of these changes and keep your file up to date. The following is a summary of the essential information you need to include on your recipe form:

- **Name of item.**

- **Recipe number**/identification within the file system.

- **Yield.** Record the total quantity that the recipe will yield.

- **Portion size.** List portions by weight or number of pieces. You may want to include what size of utensil to use for serving. For example, use the 6-oz ladle for a cup of soup.

- **Garnishes.** Be specific and make sure every plate goes out looking the same. This includes plate setup. You may want to draw a diagram or include a photograph to show your staff how the chicken should lean up against the polenta squares and how the asparagus should sit at an angle on the other side of the chicken.

- **Ingredients.** List ingredients in order. Make sure to list quantities of ingredients used, and keep the abbreviation used for quantities consistent. If you use "oz" for ounce in one recipe, make sure you use it in all your recipes. Give the physical state of ingredients: Are the nuts whole or chopped? Is the flour sifted?

- **Preparation instructions.** Be sure to include any preheating instructions. Use the correct terms for instructions. Do you want the eggs mixed into the batter or folded into it? Should the employee stir or mix with an electric mixer? Be sure to include any precautions or special instructions. If someone is preparing caramel, for example, caution the individual that the sugar water is extremely hot and that they should take the mixture off the heat before adding the cream. This section should also include pan sizes, preparation time, cooking temperature, cooking time, how to test for doneness and instructions for portioning.

- **Finishing.** Describe any finish that the product needs, such as brushing with oil or melted chocolate drizzled on top. In addition, include how to cool and at what temperature the product should be held. Can it sit at room temperature or does it need to be refrigerated?

- **Cost.** Not all restaurants include cost on the recipes. If you do, the recipe can be used as a resource for everyday ordering as well as menu design. Include every ingredient and every garnish for accuracy. You will need to look at product invoices to get unit prices, then determine the ingredient cost from this. Total the cost of each ingredient for your total recipe cost. Divide by the number of portions to come up with the portion cost.

The following page has an example of a standardized recipe card:

RECIPE NO. 126   NAME: BLUE RIDGE JAMBALAYA

Portion size: 1.5 cups   Yields: 40 portions

Cost Per Portion: 0.90

Ingredients	Weight/Measure	Cost
Chicken, boneless breast cut in 1-inch pieces	4 lbs	$8.00
Andouille sausage, sliced	2 lbs	$5.58
Celery, chopped	16 cups	$3.16
Red peppers, chopped	8 each	$6.00
Onions, chopped	4 each	$0.40
Garlic cloves, minced	8 each	$0.17
Short-grain brown rice, dry	6 cups	$4.74
Beer	32 oz	$3.50
Chicken stock	60 oz	$1.72
Canned diced tomato	60 oz	$2.12
Tabasco sauce	4 tsp	$0.03
Parsley (garnish)		$0.04
Cornbread (side)		$0.58

TOTAL COST $36.04

Directions:

Trim chicken and cut into 1-inch pieces. Heat vegetable oil in a large sauté pan. Add chicken and cook through. Add sausage and heat through.

In a large stockpot, sauté onion, garlic, celery and red pepper in oil. Add rice and coat rice with oil. Turn heat down to low, add beer and broth a little at a time, allowing the rice to absorb the liquid before adding more. When rice has simmered about 15-20 minutes, add tomato, chicken and sausage. Continue cooking until done and rice is tender (about 1 hour). Add Tabasco, salt and pepper.

Portion out the jambalaya into smaller containers to cool. Can refrigerate or use immediately for service.

Service:

Serve in a dinner bowl using a 1.5-cup ladle with a piece of cornbread on the side. Top with parsley.

Yield Costs

Once you have standardized recipes in place, you can determine the per-plate cost of every dish. In order to do this, you need to know the basic ingredients' cost and the edible yield of those ingredients for each dish. There are a number of terms you need to be familiar with in order to be able to determine yield costs:

- **As-Purchased (AP) Weight.** The weight of the product as delivered including bones, trim, etc.

- **Edible-Portion (EP) Weight.** The amount of weight or volume that is available to be portioned after carving or cooking.

- **Waste.** The amount of usable product that is lost due to processing, cooking or portioning as well as usable by-products that have no salable value.

- **Usable Trim.** Processing by-products that can be sold as other menu items. These recover a portion or all of their cost.

- **Yield.** The net weight or volume of food after processing but before portioning.

- **Standard Yield.** The yield generated by standardized recipes and portioning procedures (e.g., how much usable product remains after processing and cooking).

- **Standard Portion.** The size of the portion according to the standardized recipe, also the basis for determining the cost of the plated portion.

- **Yield Cost.** What a product yields is dependent on

how much your cooks may have to trim down. The yield cost, therefore, is the cost of the actual product that is put on the plate. This often is different than what you pay the vendor for a particular item.

- **Convenience foods.** Items where at least a portion of the preparation labor is done before delivery can cut your labor costs. These can include pre-cut chicken, ready-made dough, etc. The food cost of convenience foods are higher than if you made them from scratch, but once you factor in labor, necessary equipment, inventories of ingredients, more complicated purchasing, storage, etc., you may find that these foods offer considerable savings.

- **Costing convenience foods.** To cost convenience foods, you simply count, weigh or measure the portion size and determine how many portions there are. Then divide the number of servable portions into the AP price. Even with their pre-preparation, a small allowance for normal waste must be factored in. This amount is often as little as 2 percent per yield.

- **Costing items from scratch is a little more complex.** Most menu items require processing that causes shrinkage of some kind. As a result, if the weight or volume of the cooked product is less than the AP weight, the EP cost will be higher than the AP price. The calculation is a simple addition of the labor involved and the amount of salable product being reduced. Through this process, your buyer uses yields to determine quantities to purchase and your chef discovers optimum quantities to order that result in the highest yield and the least waste.

- **Update your menu item costs at least once a month.** Remember, fresh produce and seafood prices particularly can fluctuate wildly. Appropriate software will track these changes for you.

- **Compare menu prices to menu item costs on a regular basis.** This way you will know when you need to change menu prices to reflect increased food costs (the cost of food, like most things, has a tendency to increase over time). If you monitor your cost and prices, you will be able to change prices before your profits begin to spiral downwards.

Menu Pricing

Menu pricing is a major component of your food cost equation. The more you can charge your customers, the lower your food-cost percentage. Pricing may seem like a mathematical exercise or a lucky guess, but it is neither of these. Pricing is based on a markup of cost, which is figured by determining food cost, sales history and profit margin. But pricing strategy does not end there. Consider the following:

- **Pricing decisions.** They are influenced by indirect factors such as:
  - Human psychology
  - Market conditions
  - Location
  - Atmosphere
  - Service style
  - Competition
  - Customers' willingness to pay

- **Never forget that prices are demand or market driven.** When the economy is poor, restaurants are likely to see reduced profits because people may be eating out and traveling less. The market will ultimately be a large determinant of your prices. In the end, what it costs you to produce a particular menu item will not matter if the price is so high that no one will buy it. Make sure that your prices reflect not only the cost of the item but also what the competition is charging and what the customer is willing to spend on an item.

- **Price competitively.** Market-driven prices are more responsive to competition. Menu items that are common in an area (hamburgers, chicken sandwiches, prime rib and French fries) and can be purchased at many restaurants and have to be priced competitively.

- **Don't allow chefs to determine pricing.** The plates your chefs create are their pride and joy, but don't let chefs set the prices.

- **Signature dishes.** Focus on prices that are demand driven; your profitability will be higher. Dishes that have demand-driven prices may be signature items or simply items that are hot food trends.

- **Location and atmosphere are also important in determining menu prices.** If you buy red snapper in Seattle, the price you expect to pay as a customer is greater than what you would expect to pay for the same dinner in Athens, Georgia. Likewise, if you purchase a grilled chicken sandwich at a restaurant with table service, you expect to pay more than if you get this meal at a drive-through restaurant.

- **Keep an eye on the competition.** Check out what the competition is charging. If you are serving the exact same item as the diner down the street for $3 more, you will invariably lose customers to the other diner, all other things being equal.

- **Customers' willingness to pay.** This is very important when making pricing decisions. All the other factors make no difference if your customers think your prices are too high for what they are receiving. Remember, your customers aren't concerned with your costs. They are concerned with getting their money's worth when they dine out.

How Indirect Factors Can Help Increase Profits

Certain factors can give you a competitive edge, allowing you to charge more than the competition for your products. For instance, if you operate a steak house that serves prime beef and all the other steak houses in town serve choice and select, you are able to charge more for your product because of the higher quality. Other factors may allow you to charge more (or less) as well. If your steak house has lush decorations and the service is impeccable or if you have off-street or valet parking, you offer amenities that allow you to charge higher prices than some of your competition may be able to. Make the most of the following:

- **Plate presentation.** Introduce flair! Good plate presentations will allow higher prices than a plate that was given no thought as to its appearance. If the customer is served a plate that looks good, with thought given to garnishes, arrangement and color, he or she will be willing to pay more than if the food is scattered on the plate and hurried out of the kitchen.

- **Serve food on china and use nice glassware.** It will add value to the meal, enabling you to charge more than if you served meals in baskets, use plastic or Styrofoam.

- **Atmosphere and décor.** Consider remodeling your restaurant if it has not been updated for a number of years. Would just a fresh coat of paint spruce up your dining room and make it an attractive, comfortable place for a meal?

- **Cleanliness.** Customers do not want to eat in a restaurant that is dirty, nor do they want to eat with utensils that have not been properly cleaned. Keep a regular cleaning schedule (and pest control schedule!). Make sure your restaurant is an attractive venue.

- **Service.** What type of service do you offer? While your customers definitely want quality food, good service is just as important.

- **Table service.** Focus more on table service. It always allows you to charge higher menu prices than carryout or self-service.

- **Location.** Where are you located? This is an important factor in determining what you will be able to charge. If you are in a middle-class neighborhood, you won't want your prices to be on the cutting edge, even if your food is. If you are in a more urban environment, you can probably do both.

- **What is your customer base?** If your customers are college students, you know they have limited spending budgets. Don't price yourself out of the market.

Calculating Entrée and Meal Food Cost

Armed with cost information, you are now in a position to establish your menu prices. Remember, however, that prices will also have to take indirect factors into consideration.

- **Calculate food costs.** Usually food cost is expressed as a percentage of the menu price or of overall sales. Food cost of a specific menu item is figured by dividing the cost of the ingredients for the item by the menu price. This figure is expressed as a percentage. For example: $3.80 (ingredient food cost) ÷ $12.50 (selling price) = .30 (30-percent food cost).

- **Record overall food costs on a monthly income statement.** These numbers will help you decide how well your restaurant operation is doing.

- **Use your monthly figures.** High monthly food costs can be an indication of many things: the need for employee training, the need to adjust menu prices to reflect costs better, over-purchasing, waste and theft to name but a few.

- **Set targets.** Define realistic food cost targets for your establishment.

- **Determine the revenue you can make from an item.** Look at the cost, the menu price and your sales history. If you divide the total income into the total cost of the item, you can determine food cost for a particular period of time. For example, if you sold 200 items during a month that had a cost of $3.80 and price of $12.50: $760 (cost of $3.80 multiplied by 200) ÷ $2500 (sold 200 at $12.50) = 30%.

- **Use your sales history to forecast which items will sell in the future.** It can help you evaluate how much to purchase and prepare. It can even help you reduce kitchen labor costs.

- **Poor menu design?** If you're not reaching your food-cost goals or are not achieving as high a profit margin as you would like, it may be because of your menu design. Are you emphasizing high food costs or low profit items? Change the design of your menu. It will help decrease food cost and increase profits. Remember, if you sell too many high-cost items, your food cost will go up because many of these (such as beef and seafood) have a high cost. On the other hand, if you sell too many low-cost items, your check averages and gross profits will decline. When designing your menu, you will want to have a mix of both of these types of items.

- **Keep in mind that there's a difference between actual food cost and target food cost.** Every restaurant has a food-cost percentage or a food-cost percentage range that they strive to obtain based on a determined weighted food-cost calculation. Often, managerial bonuses are tied to reaching such food-cost goals.

- **Moving targets.** It's a month-to-month battle to keep your ever-changing food costs in your target area. Just remember, your actual food cost is what you actually spend on ingredients. While your target food costs may be 32 percent, last March your actual food costs might have been 38 percent. Identify the reasons for this difference; it's an important factor in controlling food costs.

Math and Costing Software

The industry generally uses five different pricing methods. The pros and cons of each method are discussed below.

The five methods are as follows:
1. Food-cost percentage pricing
2. Factor pricing

3. Actual cost pricing
4. Gross profit pricing
5. Prime cost pricing

- **What you'll need.** To use these methods you will need to gather certain pieces of information from the following sources:
  - Sales history and daily receipts
  - Production sheets
  - Profit and loss statements

- **Costing software.** Software will make all of your calculations easier and more accurate. Atlantic Publishing offers a program called NutraCoster. NutraCoster will calculate product cost (including labor, packaging and overhead) and nutritional content. The program costs about $300 and can be ordered online at www.atlantic-pub.com or by calling 800-541-1336. In addition, Atlantic Publishing offers a software program called ChefTec, software for inventory control, recipe, menu costing and nutritional analysis.

Food Cost Percentage Pricing

This is probably the most widely used method of menu pricing and more than likely it will be the way you price the majority of your menu items. To calculate cost percentages, use *target food-cost percentage* and *actual item food cost.*

- **How it works.** With the food-cost percentage method, you determine what percentage of sales will be taken by overhead, labor and food cost and what percentage can be profit. Most restaurants want to realize a profit between 10 and 20 percent, but each establishment is different, so you'll need to determine what your actual and target percentages are.

- **The calculation.** To determine prices with this method, you must know your actual food cost and your target food cost percentage: Food cost ÷ target food cost percentage = menu price.

- **Example.** Let's say you have a Chicken Caesar Salad on your menu. Its food cost is $1.84 and your establishment's target food cost is 35 percent. Therefore: $1.84 ÷ 0.35 = $5.25.

- **Round up or down.** The price, in the above example, is actually $5.26, but round to 5 or a 9 when setting your prices. You could also round up to $5.35, if you feel your customers will pay this amount for this item. Most restaurant mangers tend to round figures up.

- **Pros.** It's an easy formula to use.

- **Cons.** It doesn't take labor or other costs into consideration.

Factor Pricing

As with cost-percentage pricing, factoring also uses your overall target food cost (as a percentage) and the particular item's food cost to determine price. To calculate the price factor, use *target food cost percentage* and *actual item food cost.*

- **How it works.** This method uses a factor that represents food-cost percentage. To determine prices with this method, the food cost is multiplied by the pricing factor. The factor will always be the percentage of your desired food cost divided by 100.

- **The calculation.** Let's say your target food cost is 35 percent. Divide 35 into 100, and you get 2.86 as your factor. By multiplying this number by your food cost, you come up with a price: $100 \div 35 = 2.86$.

- **Example.** If the food cost on a dish is $2.67: $2.67 x 2.86 = $7.65. (food cost x pricing factor = menu price).

- **Pros.** It's an easy method.

- **Cons.** Each individual item will not meet your overall target food cost. Some of your menu items will have a higher cost and some will have a lower cost. Factoring will overprice high-cost items and underprice low-cost items.

Actual-Cost Pricing

This method is used when the menu price is established before the food cost is known. By looking at all other costs, it determines what can be spent of food cost. This method includes profit as part of the menu price. Catering operations use it when working with a customer who has a definite budget that they have to meet. By working back from what the person can spend, the manager can determine what can be spent on food and, in turn, what kind of menu they can offer the customer. To calculate actual costs, use *menu price, overhead costs* (as a percentage), *labor costs* (as a percentage) and *desired profits* (as a percentage).

- **How it works.** First, you need to determine what percentage of your costs go into overhead and labor and what percentage of sales need to go to profit. Since this equation is expressed as a percentage, overhead, labor, food cost and profit must equal 100 percent: 100% - overhead % - labor % - profit % = food cost %.

- **The calculation.** By looking at your profit and loss statement you see that your labor is 30 percent of your sales, overhead is 20 percent and you know you are aiming for a 15-percent profit: 100% - 30% - 20% - 15% = 35%. Therefore, you can spend 35 percent of the price you establish on food cost.

- **Example.** Look at your sales history. Let's say you earned $100,000 in a 6-month period. Of that $100,000, $30,000 was spent on labor; $20,000 was spent on overhead expenses and $15,000 was allocated to profit. That leaves you $35,000 to spend on food.

- **Let's look at a specific menu item now.** Your lasagna sells for $11. Of that $11, $3.30 is spent on labor; $2.20 is spent on overhead and $1.65 is profit. That leaves you $3.85 to spend on food.

- **Pros.** It includes profit in the calculation of the price of each menu item.

- **Cons.** You are working backward from menu price to food cost, so this method may not be helpful if your goal is to come up with menu prices in the first place.

Gross Profit Pricing

The gross profit method is designed to enable you to make a certain amount in profit from each customer. To calculate gross profits, use *past revenue* in dollars, *past gross profit* in dollars, *past number of customers* and *item actual food cost*.

- **How it works.** Let's say your food service operation looks at its past year's sales and you find that you made $80,000 in sales. Food cost was $25,600, so your gross profit was $54,400 (no costs other than food have been subtracted at this point, so this is not net profit). From your guest check tally, you can conclude that you served 25,000 customers during that time period.

- **The calculation.** Divide the gross profit by the number of customers and an average gross profit of $3.20 per customer is established: Gross profit ($54,400) ÷ number of customers (25,000) = average gross profit per customer ($2.18).

- **Next, establish your food cost from your stan- dardized recipe.** This added to the gross profit to determine your selling price: Food cost + average gross profit = selling price.

- **Example.** Say your lasagna's food cost is $3.85: $3.85 + $2.18 = $6.03.

- **Pros.** You are assured of making a predetermined amount of money on each customer. It works well when customer counts are predictable.

- **Cons.** It is hard to adjust for any major changes in business or customer counts; it may be more adaptable for institutional operations like hospitals and schools than for commercial establishments. It does not take the cost of labor into account.

Prime Cost Pricing

Items on your menu will differ with regards to how much labor is involved in their production. Homemade soups and desserts, for instance, involve quite a bit more labor than premade items. This method allows the price to reflect this labor cost.

- **Calculate labor costs.** Labor expenditure can be determined by noting the length of time that each item takes to prepare. This labor figure should include the time it takes to assemble ingredients and utensils, washing, chopping, peeling, mixing, preliminary cooking (such as blanching) and cleanup time. The labor cost is determined by taking this amount of time and multiplying it by the employee's hourly wage: Employee wage x amount of time to prepare = labor cost of producing item.

- **Labor cost of individual servings.** In order to determine a labor cost for each serving of a particular item, simply divide the above number by the number of portions. When this amount is added to the food cost, you come up with your prime food cost.

- **To calculate prime costs, use the following figures:** *Total labor cost* as a percentage, *labor cost for preparing item, actual item food cost* and *target food cost* as a percentage.

- **How it works.** Look at your menu and determine which items require an extensive amount of labor in the production process. Then determine the labor used to prepare the specific menu items and add the items' food cost to the labor cost to get a total: Food cost + labor cost = item cost.

- **Next,** determine what percentage the labor cost for preparing the item is of your total labor percentage. This number will be expressed as a percentage. Add the item's labor percentage to your target food cost (expressed as a percentage) to come up with the prime food-cost percentage.

- **The last step.** Divide the total item cost by the prime food-cost percentage and you get the menu selling price.

- **Example.** Your menu includes a meat lasagna. It takes your prep cook 1.5 hours to prepare 2 trays of 12 servings. Your prep cook is paid $8 an hour (since the line cook does not have to do anything but reheat the lasagna, that labor does not have to be figured in). Labor for this item is $12. For each portion, the cost is 50 cents: $8 x 1.5 = $12 and $12 ÷ 24 = $0.50.

- **Item labor cost.** By looking at your financial statements you know that your total labor is 25 percent, so you figure out that the labor for this item is 8 percent. Add this percentage to your desired food cost (say 37 percent) for the prime food-cost percentage: 8% + 37%= 45%.

- **Suggested menu price.** Direct labor percent + desired food-cost percent = prime food-cost percent. Now, add the direct labor per portion (50 cents) to the food cost (say $4) and divide this by the prime food-cost percentage (45 percent). This will give you a suggested menu price: Direct labor per portion + food cost per portion ÷ prime food-cost percent =

suggested menu price: ($0.50 + $4 ÷ .45) = $10. In reality, this would probably be adjusted to $9.95.

- **Pros.** You can include cost for labor on items that require a significant amount of labor in the preparation.

- **Cons.** It is a complicated method to use. It should only be used on items with a high labor cost.

Additional Ways to Determine Prices

Prices are generally determined by competition and demand. Your prices must be in line with the category in which customers place you. You want your customers to know that your image and your prices fit into that picture. Here are four ways to determine prices:

- **Competitive pricing.** This method is simply based on meeting or beating your competitions' prices. This is an ineffective method, since it assumes diners are making their choice on price alone and not food quality, ambiance, service, etc.

- **Intuitive pricing.** This means you don't want to take the time to find out what your competition is charging, so you are charging based on what you feel guests are willing to pay. If your sense of the value of your product is good, then it works. Otherwise, it can be problematic.

- **Psychological pricing.** Price is more of a factor to lower-income customers who go to lower-priced restaurants. If they don't know an item is good, they assume it is if it's expensive. If you change your prices, the order in which buyers see them also affects their perceptions. If an item was initially more expensive, it will be viewed as a bargain and vice versa.

- **Trial-and-error pricing.** This is based on customer reactions to prices. It is not practical in terms of determining your overall prices, but can be effective with individual items to bring them closer to the price a customer is willing to pay, or to distinguish them from similar menu items with a higher or lower food cost.

Other Factors That Will Help You Determine Prices

Whether customers view you as a leader or a follower can make a big difference regarding how they view your prices. If people think of you as the best seafood restaurant in the area, they'll be willing to pay a little more. Here are some other considerations:

- **Service determines people's sense of value.** This is even truer when the difference in actual food quality between you and the competition is negligible. If your customers order at a counter and bus their own tables, this lack of service cost needs to be reflected in your prices. Also, in a competitive market, providing great service can be a factor that puts you in a leadership position and allows you to charge a higher price.

- **Other considerations.** Location, ambiance, customer base, product presentation and desired check average all factor into what you feel you can charge and what you need to charge to make a profit.

Menu Sales Analysis

Menu sales analysis, or menu scores, track how many of each menu item is sold. Looking at this information, together with food cost and menu prices, can give the food service manager a great deal of information. Look at the following:

- **Sales mix.** Study the menu sales mix. Determine which menu items should be emphasized.

- **Emphasize the mix of items and keep your food costs under control.** Concentrating on the mix is one of the best ways to realize the highest profit possible. Rather than focusing on the profit of individual menu items, you should concentrate on what kind of profit you are achieving from your menu as a whole.

- **Avoid negatively impacting your check average.** In an attempt to contain food costs, don't emphasize only low-cost items. Usually items that have a low food cost also have a low menu price (items such as chicken and vegetarian meals). If your customers predominantly are buying these items, your check average will be too low to realize the profit you desire.

Analysis Simplified

Managers have different ways of analyzing their sales mix. This may range from simply looking at a cash register report at the end of each night, to having an intuitive feeling for which items are selling, to creating a complicated way of categorizing each menu item in order to analyze the sales mix. Some of these methods focus on controlling food costs to increase profitability and others focus on increasing sales of more profitable items. While the more complicated methods have their advantages, most food service managers are hard pressed for time and more than likely you can't squeeze even one more hour out of their week to analyze menu sales. The following guidelines represent a middle ground. You can still get the information you need from a sales analysis, but you don't have to devote a great deal of time to computation:

- **Menu sales mix.** When you're looking at your menu sales mix, you are interested in three things:
    1. How many of an item are sold
    2. Item cost
    3. Item profitability

- **Why is the sales mix so important?** Assume a restaurant serves only two products:
    1. Shrimp with a total food cost of $5 and a selling price of $12.
    2. Chicken breast with a total food cost of $2.50 and a selling price of $8.50.

WEEK 1 (1,000 Entrees Sold)

900 Shrimp Dinners	
Sales	(900 x $12) = $10,800
Cost of Sales	(900 x $5) = $4,500
100 Chicken Breasts	
Sales	(100 x $8.50) = $850
Cost of Sales	(100 x $2.50) = $250
Total Items Sold	= 1,000
Total Sales	= $11,650
Total Cost of Sales	= $4,750
$4,750 ÷ $11,650 x 100	= 40% Food Cost

NET PROFIT = $6,900 AND 40% FOOD COST

Now examine the second week with the reverse sales mix.

WEEK 2 (1,000 Entrees Sold)

900 Chicken Breasts	
Sales	(900 × $8.50) = $7,650
Cost of Sales	(900 × $2.50) = $2,250
100 Shrimp Dinners	
Sales	(100 × $12) = $1,200
Cost of Sales	(100 × $5) = $500
Total Items Sold	= 1,000
Total Sales	= $8,850
Total Cost of Sales	= $2,750
$2,750 ÷ $8,850 × 100	= 31% Food Cost

NET PROFIT = $6,100 AND 31% FOOD COST

In the previous example, Week One had a 12-percent higher profit margin with the same number of customers served. Yet the food-cost percentage was 9-percent higher than in Week Two. Thus, in this simplified example, you can clearly see the effect the weighted average sales has on food-cost percentages and overall profitability.

- **Food-cost percentage meaning.** Don't become overly concerned over food-cost percentages; they are truly meaningless unless you know what your food-cost percentage should be for the given time in question. Remember, you get paid in and deposit dollars into the bank, not percentages.

- **Food-costs percentages are different at individual establishments.** There are establishments in this country that can run a 50-percent or higher food-cost percentage and still be very profitable because of the high sales volume.

Analyze and Classify Your Menu Sales Mix

Once you have an effective menu design, analyzing your sales mix to determine the impact each item has on sales, costs and profits is an important practice. If you have costs and waste under control, looking at your menu sales mix can help you further reduce costs and boost profits. You will find that some items need to be promoted more aggressively, while others need to be dropped altogether. Classifying your menu items is necessary for making those decisions.

- **You need to know the answers to these questions:**
    1. What is the most popular entrée served?

    2. What is the most profitable entrée served by dollar amount?

    3. What is the lowest food-cost item served by percentage of food cost?

Food suppliers are a vital part of your restaurant operation.

CHAPTER FOUR

PURCHASING

The goal of purchasing is to obtain wholesome, safe foods to meet your menu requirements. The operation must have food to serve customers when needed. The food needs to be the right quality consistent with the operation's standards and purchased at the lowest possible cost.

- **Vendors and food safety.** Food safety at this step is primarily the responsibility of your vendors. It's your job to choose your vendors wisely.

- **Suppliers must meet federal and state health standards.** They should use the HACCP system in their operations and train their employees in sanitation.

- **Delivery trucks.** Delivery trucks should have adequate refrigeration and freezer units, and foods should be packaged in protective, leak-proof, durable packaging. Let vendors know upfront what you expect from them. Put food-safety standards in your purchase specification agreements. Ask to see their most recent board of health sanitation reports, and tell them you will be inspecting trucks on a quarterly basis.

- **Delivery schedules.** Good vendors will cooperate with your inspections and should adjust their delivery schedules to avoid your busy periods so that incoming foods can be received and inspected properly.

- **Your inventory system is the critical component of purchasing.** Before placing an order with a supplier, you need to know what you have on hand and how much will be used. Allow for a cushion of inventory so you won't run out between deliveries. Once purchasing has been standardized, the manager simply orders from your suppliers. Records show supplier, prices, unit of purchase, product specifications, etc. This information needs to be kept on paper and preferably computerized. Purchase food items according to usage. For example, if you plan to use tomatoes by blending and mixing them with other ingredients to make a sauce, purchase broken tomatoes as opposed to whole tomatoes. However, if you intend to use tomatoes to decorate a dinner plate or as a topping, opt for high-quality produce, such as baby plum vine-grown tomatoes.

Inventory Levels

The first step in computing what item to order and how much you need is to determine the inventory level, or the amount needed on hand at all times. This is a simple procedure, but it requires order sheets. To determine the amount you need to order, you must first know the amount you have in inventory. Walk through the storage areas and mark in the "On Hand" column the amounts that are there. To determine the "Build to Amount," you will need to know when regularly scheduled deliveries arrive for that item and the amount used in the period between deliveries. Add on about 15 percent to the average amount used; this will cover unexpected usage, a late delivery or a backorder from the vendor. The amount you need to order is the difference between the "Build to Amount" and the amount "On Hand." Experience and food demand will reveal the amount an average order should contain. By purchasing too little, the restaurant may run out of supplies before the next delivery. Ordering too much will result in tying up money and putting a drain on the restaurant's cash flow. Buying up items in large amounts can save money, but you must consider the cash-flow costs.

- **A buying schedule** should be set up and adhered to. This would consist of a calendar showing:
  - Which day's orders need to be placed.

  - When deliveries will be arriving.

  - What items will be arriving from which company.

  - Phone numbers of sales representatives to contact for each company.

  - The price the sales representative quoted.

- **Post the buying schedule on the office wall.** When a delivery doesn't arrive as scheduled, the buyer should place a phone call to the salesperson or company immediately. Don't wait until the end of the day when offices are closed.

- **A Want Sheet may be placed on a clipboard in the kitchen.** This sheet is made available for employees to write in any items they may need to do their jobs more efficiently. This is a very effective form of communication; employees should be encouraged to use it. The buyer should consult this sheet every day. A request might be as simple as a commercial-grade carrot peeler. If, for example, the last one broke and the preparation staff has been using the back of a knife instead, the small investment could save you from an increase in labor and food costs.

ITEM	EMPLOYEE	APPROVED	ORDERED ON	RECEIVED

Purchasing and Ordering

What exactly is the difference? Purchasing is setting the policy on which suppliers, brands, grades and varieties of products will be ordered. These are your standardized purchase specifications; the specifics of how items are delivered, paid for and returned. These specifications are negotiated between management and distributors. Basically, purchasing is what you order and from whom. Ordering, then, is simply the act of contacting the suppliers and notifying them of the quantity you require. This is a simpler, lower-level task. Here are the basics:

- **Develop a purchasing program.** Once menus have been created that meet your customers' satisfaction and your profit needs, develop a purchasing program that ensures your profit margins.

- **An efficient purchasing program incorporates:** Standard purchase specifications based on standardized recipes, and standardized yields and portion control that allow for accurate costs based on portions actually served.

- **Keep in mind:** Purchasing more than you need usually results in poor portioning, excess spoilage, waste and theft. Not buying enough can mean paying retail prices, or using a more expensive substitute.

- **Purchasing procedures.** These procedures should include creating written purchasing specifications for every product and selecting good, reliable purveyors.

Your purchasing program should do three things:

1. Allow you to purchase the required items at prices that meet your food cost goals.

2. Maintain control over your existing inventory.

3. Establish a set of procedures to be sure that you receive quality product at the best price.

- **Purchasing responsibility.** Either take on the purchasing yourself or assign a specific employee to do it. Make sure that this person keeps current with ever-changing food prices.

- **Price checks for different vendors.** Sometimes you may find that one vendor is less expensive than another for a while, and then this may shift. Keep current with competing vendors' prices.

Purchasing Specifications

By creating purchasing specifications, you can control which items you purchase and you can maintain product consistency. This information is extremely important if you have more than one person that does ordering in your operation. You need to record the following basic information:

- **Purchasing specifications.** They state the exact requirements for the amount and quality of items purchased. These specifications should include:
  - Product name
  - Quantity to be purchased (designated with correct unit such as pounds, can size, etc.)
  - Indication of grade, if applicable
  - Unit by which prices are quoted
  - What the product will be used to produce

- **Meats.** Meats should be inspected by the USDA or other appropriate agency. The parts or packaging should carry a federal or state inspection stamp.

- **Eggs.** Eggs should have a USDA grade; frozen and dried eggs should be pasteurized.

- **Shellfish.** Shellfish should be purchased from suppliers that appear on public health service Food and Drug Administration lists of Certified Shellfish Shippers or on lists of state-approved sources. The control tags must be available if live shellfish are used.

- **Introduce a record sheet.** Make it readily available for all your employees. They need to be sure that they're ordering the correct items in the correct amounts. You're also more likely to attain your desired food cost by keeping these records and maintaining purchasing controls. Keeping your food cost down will help you to maximize profits from your menu prices. The following form illustrates an example of a purchasing specification form:

Item	Quantity	Unit	Pricing Unit	Unit Price	Amount
Canned diced tomato	4	#10 cans	Case	$10.83	$43.32
Shredded provolone cheese	10	Pounds	Pounds	$4.55	$45.50

Purchasing and Inventory Software

Purchasing and inventory software is readily available to restaurant operators. Many larger organizations are using inventory control software that saves a significant amount of time and money. Most managers are used to the monthly grind, standing in the walk-ins counting eggs, butter pats and frozen chickens. With inventory control software, managers can use a laser scanner, similar to the ones used in grocery stores, to scan bar codes. The software can also be linked to your distributors and you can place your orders electronically based on the inventory. Check out the following software vendors:

- **Atlantic Publishing** (www.atlantic-pub.com; 800-541-1336) offers a software program called ChefTec, software for inventory control, recipe, menu costing and nutritional analysis.

- **Visit the National Restaurant Association's Web site** at www.restaurant.org for vendors of this software (as well as many other products). Take a trip to their annual National Restaurant Association Exhibit each year in Chicago to see all the latest products available in the restaurant industry.

- **EZ Stock.** You can see one version of the inventory software on Johnson Technologies' Web site at www.johnsontech.com. According to their Web site, EZ Stock can be purchased for $25 a month per module for a minimum of one year.

- **Another Web site of interest is www.foodprofile.com.** This site was established for the collection and distribution of product information for the food industry and is part of an initiative called Efficient Foodservice Response (EFR). Distributors pay to list their products on this site. It provides over 65,000 items and has the most up-to-date product information available, including serving suggestions, nutritional information, cooking instructions and ingredient statements. EFR is an industry-wide initiative to improve efficiency in the purchasing process. To find out more about EFR, log on to www.efr-central.com.

- **Consider placing your orders online.** Almost all distributors now have systems in place to order online. The advantages are numerous: it reduces ordering errors, it's convenient, there may be discounts, and most systems build a customer database based on what you have previously ordered making re-orders easy. A list of vendor Web sites follows:
  - www.usfoodservice.com
  - www.sysco.com
  - www.seafax.com/cgi-bin/WebObjects/Seafax
  - winebusiness.com
  - www.tampamaid.com
  - www.foodservicecentral.com
  - www.foodservice.com
  - www.fbix.com
  - www.buyproduce.com
  - www.agribuys.com
  - www.alliantfs.com
  - www.gfs.com
  - www.nugget.com
  - www.pyamonarch.com
  - www.pocahontasfoods.com
  - www.whitetoque.com
  - www.syscono.com

- **Use written purchase orders (PO).** A PO is a written authorization for a vendor to supply goods or services at a specified price over a specified time period.

Acceptance of the PO constitutes a purchase contract and is legally binding on all parties. Utilizing POs will enable you to know what was ordered, the quantity, and the price. If you are using software to record the invoice and receipt of inventory, the program will restock and adjust pricing automatically. In addition, your perpetual inventory will be updated. Purchase orders from software programs can easily be faxed or e-mailed into the vendor, saving time and money.

- **When purchasing food, avoid more expensive name brands wherever possible.** Of course, you want to make sure you're buying quality ingredients for your food, but are your customers really likely to tell the difference between a "name brand" and an "industrial brand"?

- **Local growers.** Talk to local fresh-produce suppliers to see if you can't get fresher, cheaper, better-quality fresh produce direct from the grower. Why pay a supplier to get the fruit and vegetables that are shipped to their central warehouse, then shipped back to you, when you can just drive 10 minutes down the road and enjoy food right off the tree or vine? You can also use this as a promotional device. If you use local produce, let your customers know!

- **Cooperative purchasing.** Many restaurants have formed cooperative purchasing groups to increase their purchasing power. The cooperatives purchase items that are commonly used by all food service operators. By joining together to place large orders, restaurants can usually get substantial price reductions. Some organizations even purchase their own trucks and warehouses and hire personnel to pick up deliveries. This can be advantageous for restaurants that are in the proximity of a major supplier or shipping center. Many items, such as produce, dairy products, seafood and meat, may be purchased this way. Chain restaurants have a centralized purchasing department and, often, large self-distribution centers.

- **Make sure you shop for purveyors.** Don't rest once you've found one. Comparison shop on a continual basis.

- **Look at vendors' product labels for box strength.** This will tell you where the product came from. Most manufacturers won't ship more than 100 miles away from their plants. The further away that a supplier is located, the more shipping will cost.

- **Consider planting your own herb and/or vegetable garden.** Great food starts with using the freshest herbs and vegetables and the best way to do that is to grow them yourself! The techniques for growing your own are not difficult. With a little planning, you can build your own 24-hour supply of garden-fresh herbs. Even a small garden can infuse your kitchen with heavenly aromas and striking flavor. What a great way to lower your food cost and separate yourself from the competition! You can buy seeds online at:
  - www.burpee.com/main.asp
  - www.dansgardenshop.com
  - www.johnnyseeds.com/catalog/index.html
  - www.richters.com
  - www.parkseed.com

Inventory, Storage and Accounts Payable

Ordering effectively is impossible unless you are completely familiar with the inventory items. Prior to orders being placed with vendors, counts of stock need to be established. Software programs are able to determine order quantities based upon par balances and sale figures; we highly recommend this implementation. Whether your ordering system is performed with a pencil and paper or by computer, its purpose is to:

1. Provide reports of what is needed.
2. Provide reports the specified products.
3. Provide reports of vendors and contact information.
4. Provide reports of prices.
5. Provide a historical report of prices.
6. Provide a method for the ease of order placement.

Keeps these critical points about inventory in mind:

- **Inventory amounts.** The more you have in inventory, the harder it is to control.

- **Shelf life for perishables.** Meat, produce and seafood will only last 2-3 days, so do not order too much of these products at a time.

- **Excessive inventory** ties up your cash, hindering cash flow.

- **Extra food** on hand tends to lead to over-portioning and is easier for theft.

- **Inventory turnover.** Ideally, the entire food inventory should be turned every 5-8 days.

- **Vendors.** Schedule vendor representatives visits so you are not interrupted.

- **Standing orders.** Consider placing standing orders for regularly used items.

- **Consider using one "main vendor."** If you receive

most of your product from one vendor, you will spend much less time on purchasing, there will be fewer salespeople to deal with, there will be fewer deliveries each week and labor costs will be saved. You also will receive better service. As previously mentioned, most large vendors today have online ordering systems.

- **Check trade magazines** and www.foodbuy.com for rebates available from manufacturers.

- **Join a buying group** such as the one at www.foodservice.com. They have pre-negotiated manufacturer allowances available on over 10,000 food and food-related products from over 125 network suppliers from manufacturers like Sweetheart, Ecolab, Sara Lee and General Mills.

- **Warehouse buying clubs.** Check out warehouse buying clubs such as Sam's Club, samsclub.com, Costco, costco.com and Restaurant Depot, www.restaurantdepot.com.

- **Cash discounts.** Many purveyors provide cash discounts if payment is made early, such as "2/10, net 30." With this, a 2-percent discount may be taken if payment is made within 10 days. Cash discounts are worth taking; a restaurant that purchases $500,000 per year and takes a 2-percent discount will save $10,000.

- **Alternatives.** Don't automatically use fresh fruit and vegetables if canned alternatives can be used without cutting back on meal quality. Canned tomatoes, artichoke hearts, chili peppers, pears, etc., can all be used in many meals without a big loss in flavor, and the trade off is a big drop in price and spoilage rates.

Perpetual Inventory

The perpetual inventory is a check on the daily usage of your main entrée items from the freezers and walk-ins. This is for tracking expensive items, such as meat, seafood, chicken, cans of caviar, etc. When completed, the perpetual inventory will ensure that no bulk products have been pilfered from the freezer or walk-ins. Computer software programs, such as QuickBooks®, and some POS systems will track this information for you. The following is an example of a Perpetual Order Form:

ITEM		1	2	3	4	5	6	7	8	9	10	11	12	13	14	15	16	17	18	19	20	21	22	23	24	25	26	27	28	29	30	31	1
Shrimp (20)	+	5																															
(5 lbs.)	-	1																															
	=	24																															

- **List all the food items that are listed on the Sign-out Sheet and Yield Form**. In the "Size" column, list the unit size in which the item is packaged. The contents of most cases of food are packed in units such as 5-pound boxes or 2-pound bags. Meat is usually packed by the number of pieces in a case and the case's weight. The size listed on the perpetual inventory must correspond to the size the preparation cooks are signing out of the freezer and walk-ins.

- **In the "Item" column, enter the number of each item listed.** For example, if shrimp is packed in 5-pound boxes and you have two 50-pound cases, there are 20 boxes. Enter 20 in the "Item" column. Each number along the top corresponds to each day of the month. At the end of each day, count all the items on hand and enter this figure on the "=" line. Compare this figure to the "Amount Ordered or Defrosted" column on the Preparation Sheet; these amounts must be the same as the total number of each item on the "−" line. If there were any deliveries, place this total on the "+" line.

- **Theft.** Theft can occur when someone removes a box of shrimp from the case, for example. The person then reseals the case with the other boxes to hide the gap.

- **Check the invoices every day** for the items delivered that are in your perpetual inventory. Ensure that all items signed off as being delivered are actually in the storage areas. Should there be a discrepancy, check with the employee that signed the invoice. The number of items you start with (20) plus the number you received in deliveries (5), minus the amount signed out by the preparation cooks (1), must equal the number on hand (24). If there is a discrepancy, you may have a thief.

- **What to do if you suspect theft.** Should you suspect a theft in the restaurant, record the names of all employees who worked that particular day. If thefts continue to occur, a pattern may develop among the employees who were working on all the days in question. Compute the perpetual inventory or other controls you are having a problem with at different times of the day and before and after each shift. This will pinpoint the area and shift in which the theft is occurring. Sometimes, placing a notice to all employees that you are aware of a theft problem in the restaurant will resolve the problem. Make it clear that any employee caught stealing will be terminated.

Purchasing Kickbacks and Gifts

Unfortunately, the food service industry is notorious for kickbacks. It is even more unfortunate that these kickbacks or gifts are essentially paid for by you in the form of higher prices. Here are some ideas to help keep kickbacks out of your store:

- **Purchasing and receiving must be done by different employees.** The person ordering should not be the same person receiving and checking the items.

- **Kickback policy.** Develop a general policy and list it in your employee handbook that employees cannot receive anything for free from a vendor or potential vendor.

- **Change positions.** People become complacent over time; move positions around.

- **Check on prices** of expensive items like meat and seafood yourself.

Purchasing Ideas

There are many ways to curb cost. Here are a few ideas:

- **Inexpensive fish.** Turn your customers on to seafood alternatives and lower your food cost. Consider using some alternatives such as Tilapia, farm-raised salmon, fresh-water perch, Alaskan halibut, mahi-mahi, shark or skate. Skate, for example, can be purchased wholesale right now online for $1.62 per pound. The secret, of course, is to make certain it is fresh.

- **Shelled eggs.** Consider buying shelled eggs if your restaurant uses more than three cases of eggs per week. This will reduce the amount of cardboard and other packaging that must be disposed or recycled. Shelled eggs are often packaged in 5-gallon buckets that can later be reused for cleaning or maintenance.

- **Condiments.** Use refillable condiment dispensers instead of individual condiment packets for dine-in customers.

- **Cost-Watch Web site.** This site, www.cost-watch.com, helps restaurant management control labor, utility and food and beverage costs. It also offers regional reports to compare expenses and food costs in similar restaurants as well as price trend forecasts. It is a great resource for purchasing managers.

- **Join a barter club.** Bartering allows you to buy what you need and pay for it with otherwise unsold products, such as food and beverages or even catering services. Almost anything and everything can be purchased with barter services. Nationally, over 250,000 businesses are involved in barter. Check out these Web pages:
  - www.barterwww.com
  - www.barterbrokers.com
  - www.netlabs.net/biz/itex/index.htm

- **Similar ingredients.** Include menu items that are essentially made with similar ingredients as others on the menu. For example, a shrimp cocktail and shrimp pasta are two very different meals, but the ingredients are similar. These ingredients are simple, inexpensive and don't take up a lot of storage space. Having five or six other pasta sauces to offer also loads up your menu with choices without excessively increasing your inventory. This will not only allow you to buy in bulk and keep costs down, but will also lighten the load on your kitchen staff.

- **Bread baskets.** The potential for waste in bread baskets is large. Most of these come back from the table partially eaten at best. You may want to

consider giving bread baskets only if requested or
you may want to cut down on the amount served.
You should also consider including packaged items
since these can be reused. Some operators are now
serving bread only by request or they are serving one
roll or breadstick at a time from a breadbasket with
tongs.

- **Substitute premade items.** Substitute premade
  items for some items you have been making from
  scratch. You don't have to sacrifice quality to do this;
  many premade items are good. You can also start
  with a premade item and add ingredients. For
  instance, you can buy a premade salad dressing and
  add blue cheese or fresh herbs. Using these items
  will lower your food and labor costs, and you can still
  put out a quality item.

A receiving policy will help ensure the freshest products.

CHAPTER FIVE

RECEIVING

Goals

The goals of receiving are to ensure foods are fresh and safe when they enter your facility and you are receiving what you ordered and are paying for. Transfer items to proper storage as quickly as possible.

Let's look more closely at two important parts of receiving:

1. Getting ready to receive food.
2. Inspecting the food when the delivery truck arrives.

Receiving Policy

Introduce a receiving policy. Remember, it's easy to "lose" products in this part of your operation. Let's say, for example, you have no one specifically assigned to check in orders. Normally one of your line cooks will do it. Let's also say that one day your order is late and arrives in the middle of lunch rush. No one can check the order for accuracy, so they just sign for it in a hurry. If this happens, it is virtually impossible to correct any mistakes at the time. Furthermore, if your line cooks don't get to put the order away until several hours later, you will lose product because it has sat out too long and is now unsafe to serve.

Receiving Tips

There are several important guidelines to keep in mind and tasks to complete as you get ready to receive food:

- **Calibration.** Make sure all scales and thermometers are in place and calibrated.

- **Sanitary carts.** Make sure your receiving area is equipped with sanitary carts for transporting goods.

- **Plan ahead** for deliveries to ensure sufficient refrigerator and freezer space.

- **Mark all items for storage** with the date of arrival or the "use by" date.

- **Lighting.** Keep the receiving area well lit and clean to discourage pests.

- **Remove empty containers** and packing materials immediately to a separate trash area.

- **Keep all flooring clean** of food particles and debris.

- **Delivery truck.** When the delivery truck arrives, make sure it looks and smells clean and is equipped with the proper food-storage equipment. Then inspect foods immediately.

- **Check expiration dates** of milk, eggs and other perishable goods. Make sure shelf-life dates have not expired.

- **Frozen foods.** Make sure frozen foods are in airtight, moisture-proof wrappings.

- **Reject foods that have been thawed and refrozen.** Look for signs of thawing and refreezing, such as large crystals, solid areas of ice or excessive ice in containers.

- **Rejecting canned goods.** Reject cans that have any of the following: swollen sides or ends; flawed seals or seams; dents; or rust. Also reject any cans whose contents are foamy or smell bad.

- **Check the temperature** of refrigerated and frozen foods, especially eggs and dairy products, fresh meat and fish and poultry products.

- **Look for content damage** and insect infestations.

- **Rejecting dairy products.** Reject dairy, bakery and other foods delivered in flats or crates that are dirty.

- **Weighing items.** Meats, fish and most items ordered by the pound must be weighed and tagged. Food items purchased by count need to be checked and counted. All items received must be counted, weighed and date stamped. Don't deviate from this critical step.

- **Invoice accuracy.** Check the accuracy of the invoice with regard to the purchase order, specifically price, damage, quality, quantity, brands, grades and variety. Items that are not correct need to be noted and returned before the driver leaves and the driver must sign the form. The vendor's invoice also should be checked against the actual purchase order.

- **Don't let delivery people into your storage areas.**

- **Items packed in ice.** These items need to be removed from the ice prior to weighing.

- **Check animal cavities** in fish and poultry for ice.

- **Delivery personnel should be friendly,** not rushed, and professional, but not too friendly. Ensure they know that it doesn't matter if they are in a rush; you are going to check everything in and count and weigh everything prior to their leaving.

- **All food products must be date coded, rotated and put away immediately.**

- **Placed in order.** Products should be placed on the shelves in the same order as the inventory sheets and purchase order forms. This will help in inventory counting and control.

- **Determine which employees are allowed to access the storage areas.** Storage areas are prime targets for theft. Not only employee theft, but if areas aren't kept locked and secure, outside people will be able to get in and help themselves to your products.

- **Garbage can liners.** In the kitchen, consider using clear trash bag liners as another method to deter pilferage.

- **Keep your back door locked,** well lit and on an alarm system. A small viewing panel or glass with a wire-enforced panel will enable the receiving employee to see who is at the back door.

CHAPTER SIX

STORAGE

In general, there are four possible ways to store food: First, in dry storage, for longer holding of less-perishable items. Second, in refrigeration, for short-term storage of perishable items. Third, in specially designed deep-chilling units for short periods. Finally, in a freezer for longer-term storage of perishable foods. Each type of storage has its own sanitation and safety requirements.

Dry Storage

There are many items that can be held safely in a sanitary storeroom. These include canned goods, baking supplies (such as salt and sugar), grain products (such as rice and cereals) and other dry items. In addition, some fruits (such as bananas, avocados, and pears) ripen best at room temperature. Some vegetables, such as onions, potatoes and tomatoes, also store best in dry storage. A dry-storage room should be clean and orderly with good ventilation to control temperature and humidity and retard the growth of bacteria and mold. Keep in mind the following:

- **Temperature.** For maximum shelf life, dry foods should be held at 50° F, but 60-70° F is adequate for most products.

- **Wall thermometer.** Use a wall thermometer to check the temperature of your dry-storage facility regularly. See www.atlantic-pub.com for a complete selection of thermometers.

- **First in, first out (FIFO).** To ensure freshness, store opened items in tightly covered containers. Use the FIFO rotation method, dating packages and placing incoming supplies in the back so that older supplies will be used first.

- **Pests.** To avoid pest infestation and cross-contamination, clean up all spills immediately and do not store trash or garbage cans in food storage areas.

- **Keep it up.** Do not place any items—including paper products—on the floor. Make sure the bottom shelf of the dry-storage room is at least 6 inches above the ground.

- **Avoid chemical contamination.** Never use or store cleaning materials or other chemicals where they might contaminate foods! Store them, labeled, in their own section in the storeroom away from all food supplies.

Refrigerated Storage

Many commercial refrigerators are equipped with externally mounted or built-in thermometers. These are convenient when they work, but it is important to have a backup. It's a good idea to have several thermometers in different parts of the refrigerator to ensure consistent temperature and accuracy of instruments. Record the temperature of each refrigerator on a chart, preferably once a day. Here are more facts about refrigerated foods to keep in mind:

- **Fresh products.** Keep fresh meat, poultry, seafood, dairy products, most fresh fruit and vegetables and hot leftovers in the refrigerator at internal temperatures of below 40° F.

- **Shelf life.** Although no food can last forever, refrigeration increases the shelf life of most products.

- **The colder the better.** Because refrigeration slows bacterial growth, the colder food is, the safer it is.

- **Shelves.** Your refrigeration unit should contain open, slotted shelving to allow cold air to circulate around food. Do not line shelves with foil or paper.

- **Circulation.** Do not over-load the refrigerator, and be sure to leave space between items to further improve air circulation.

- **Date everything.** All refrigerated foods should be dated and properly sealed.

- **Diary products.** Store dairy products separately from foods with strong odors like onions, cabbage and seafood.

- **Cross-contamination.** To avoid cross-contamination, store raw or uncooked food away from and below prepared or ready-to-eat food.

- **Containers.** Use clean, nonabsorbent, covered containers that are approved for food storage.

- **Raw meat.** Never allow fluids from raw poultry, fish or meat to come into contact with other foods.

- **Perishable products.** Keeping perishable items at the proper temperature is a key factor in preventing food-borne illness. Check the temperature of your refrigeration unit regularly to make sure it stays below 40° F. Keep in mind that opening and closing the refrigerator door too often can affect temperature.

- **Ready-to-eat foods** are stored above raw foods, never below.

- **Stock tags.** Fresh shellfish always arrives with an identity stock tag. This information is recorded and kept on file for 90 days.

- **Check temperatures regularly.** Place thermometers in the warmest and coldest areas of refrigerators; measure and record air temperature regularly.

Deep Chilling

Deep chilling, storing foods at temperatures between 26° F and 32° F, has been found to decrease bacterial growth. This method can be used to increase the shelf life of fresh foods, such as poultry, meat, seafood and other protein items, without compromising their quality by freezing. You can deep chill foods in specially designed units or in a refrigerator set to deep-chilling temperature.

Frozen Storage

Frozen meats, poultry, seafood, fruits and vegetables and some dairy products, such as ice cream, should be stored in a freezer at 0° F to keep them fresh and safe for an extended period of time. As a rule, you should use your freezer primarily to store foods that are frozen when you receive them. Freezing refrigerated foods can damage the quality of perishable items. It's important to store frozen foods immediately. It's also important to remember that storing foods in the freezer for too long increases the likelihood of contamination and spoilage. Like your refrigeration unit, the freezer should allow cold air to circulate around foods easily. Be sure to:

- **Use moisture-proof containers.** Store frozen foods in moisture-proof material or containers to minimize loss of flavor as well as discoloration, dehydration and odor absorption.

- **Monitor temperature regularly.** Monitor temperature regularly using several thermometers to ensure accuracy and consistent temperatures. Record the temperature of each freezer on a chart. Remember that frequently opening and closing the freezer's door can raise the temperature, as can placing warm foods in the freezer.

- **Cold loss.** To minimize heat gain, open freezer doors only when necessary and remove as many items at one time as possible. You can also use a freezer "cold curtain" to help guard against heat gain.

Organize Your Storage Areas

Set up your areas (dry storage, refrigerated and freezers) so that there is a specific place for everything. Items that move quickly should be near the door if possible. Keep the door locked. Expensive items such as exotic mushrooms, saffron and wine or alcohol used in the kitchen could be stored and locked in a separate cabinet inside the store room.

- **Label the shelves.** Ordering and checking inventory will be much easier.

- **Stacking.** The improper stacking of storage containers can result in spills, breakage and worse: accidents. Ensure that if you use storage containers, they stack properly and are easily handled.

- **Shelving.** Stacking items on top of one another in

your cool room might seem to be the most productive way to utilize your limited space, but such a system makes cleaning and access to certain items very difficult. A good shelving system that is flexible enough to allow you to easily change shelf heights will not only help you make good use of space, but also make every item in your refrigerator easier to access. In addition, cleaning will be a breeze.

- **Five-gallon buckets.** When you receive deliveries like flour, sugar and salt in large five-gallon buckets, you might be able to reuse them for storing dry materials. Buckets like these are usually airtight and designed for maximum protection of the contents. Rather than tossing them, clean, re-label, and utilize them. Do not use them for ice storage, however.

- **Ice is food too.** Use a designated ice transport container such as Saf-T-Ice Tote. Ice transfer is a cross-contamination disaster waiting to happen in most food service operations. Saf-T-Ice Totes help you control this serious food-safety danger! It is made of tough, transparent, durable polycarbonate and the unit will not nest, so dirt and bacteria cannot be transmitted by stacking. The six-gallon size keeps the carrying weight at safe levels. It also features a stainless steel bail handle for easy carrying/emptying. It meets health department requirements for dedicated food service containers and it's dishwasher safe. Saf-T-Ice Totes (Item #SI-6000, $79.95 for a pack of two) can be ordered from Atlantic Publishing at www.atlantic-pub.com or by calling 800-541-1336.

Storage Spoilage Prevention

List all spoiled food on a form; detail the date spoiled, item description and the reason that it is being tossed out. This allows you to make inventory adjustments, noting whether you're ordering too much of an item, or have an equipment problem, such as an ineffective cooler.

- **Color code, label and date all food.** Using older food before newer food will ensure you keep losses to a minimum and can see any problems coming in advance. You can also use date stickers so employees know how long an item has been stored. Use dissolvable labels so that the label and adhesive dissolve in any water temperature! Daymark Food Safety Systems manufactures a line of biodegradable labels that will dissolve in under 30 seconds, leaving no sticky residue. These labels will adhere to hard plastics and stainless steel containers. The labels are FDA approved for indirect food contact and may be purchased at www.dissolveaway.com, 800-847-0101.

- **Are your coolers too cold?** Freezing, frost and freezer burn are a major source of spoilage in the kitchen, so make regular inspections of your cooler's temperature, and keep a written chart of when the last checks were performed. Use specialty thermometers for these areas. Atlantic Publishing carrys these specialty items which you can order online at www.atlantic-pub.com. Look for fluctuations or "cold points" in the cooler that differ in temperature from the rest of the area.

- **Spoilage rates.** Different qualities and brands of food may spoil at different rates from what you're used to. If you happen to change your brand or supplier on a particular line of food, make sure to keep a closer eye on the condition of your stock, taking note of any changes in freshness so that you can alter your purchasing to suit.

- **Eggs.** To keep the yokes of your eggs from breaking easily, put any eggs to be used in the coming hours out to sit at room temperature before they're used. This simple piece of advice will keep your eggs in perfect "cracking" condition and keep your wastage to a minimum. Check with local health regulations first and remember that eggs are a highly perishable item.

- **Refreezing.** Don't refreeze foods; this will take away from the taste of the food. Sometimes you may have no choice, but if you can keep food in a cooler at a refrigerated temperature and reuse it quickly, you'll be far better off.

- **Spices, sauces and marinades can be pre-prepared and stored for long periods without spoiling,** if kept at the right temperature. If a sauce or marinade requires an item with a high spoilage rate, make a large batch and freeze it in small containers to be used as needed, saving on time and money and ensuring that every meal has a consistent taste.

- **Consider a generator.** If your electricity supply went down for half a day, what would happen to your inventory? Save yourself the heartache of watching your food go to waste in the event of a utility problem by purchasing a backup generator. A small generator powerful enough to keep your cooler could save you thousands of dollars in lost assets if the unthinkable happens.

- **Monitor your walk-ins.** Monitor your walk-ins and freezers. Your alarm monitoring company may have a program to monitor the temperature in your freezer and coolers, or you can hire a company such as Food Watch, www.foodwatch.com/foodwatch.htm. Their system will accurately and remotely measure the refrigeration efficiency of walk-ins, stand-alone refrigerators or food cases. The patent-pending Compressor Watch sensor attaches to the outside of the compressor motor and monitors the amount of time it runs by sensing the field that surrounds the motor. The system can also record the amount of time the walk-in door is left open. The system works via a telephone line. You can even review the data on your own Web site.

- **Electrical failure.** If the power does not resume within 1-2 days, or if a mechanical problem hasn't been fixed, keep the freezer closed and use dry ice to keep the freezer temperatures below freezing to prevent spoilage. Locating dry ice sources and determining your needs now will save valuable time later. Consider calling other restaurants, your vendors or cold storage companies should the problem require further delays. Plan ahead now.

Issuing

Procedures for removing inventory from storage are an integral part of the cost-control process. Here are some tips on issuing as well as an example of an Issuing Sign-out Sheet.

- **Raw food.** All raw materials from which entrées are prepared, such as meat, seafood and poultry, must be issued on a daily basis.

- **Signing out.** Whenever one of these bulk items is removed from a freezer or walk-in, it must be signed out.

- **Who should issue stock?** Managers or kitchen managers should be the only ones to issue stock from storage. When a part of a case or box is removed, the weight of the portion removed must be recorded in the "Amount" column. The Sign-out Sheet should be on a clipboard affixed to the walk-in or freezer. Once the item is signed out, the weight must be placed in the "Amount Used or Defrosted" column on a Preparation Form.

ITEM	DATE	AMOUNT/WT.	EMPLOYEE
Shrimp-box	11-30	1-5lb. box	Joe B.

This will show that the items signed out were actually used in the restaurant. From this information, the kitchen director can compute a daily yield on each item prepared. This yield will show that the portions were weighed out accurately and the bulk product that was used to prepare menu items. At any one of these steps, pilferage can occur. The signing-out procedure will eliminate missed pilferage.

CHAPTER SEVEN

PRODUCTION & SERVICE

Precise portion and menu control is crucial in controlling food cost. Physical production also should be considered when looking at cost controls and menu changes. Watch your kitchen operation to see how things are working. You may need to buy some new equipment or rearrange your labor schedule to implement some of the changes that you want. Focus particularly on the following:

- **Labor.** Are you scheduling the appropriate amount of labor for shifts and prep work?

- **Recipes.** Be sure staff members are using the standardized recipes and production sheets.

- **Inventory controls.** Do you have strict inventory controls in place? Is your staff familiar with inventory procedures?

- **Invest in labor-saving equipment.** You'll be able to pay for the equipment in no time with the money that you will save on labor.

Involve the Crew

A good way to lower food costs is to involve your kitchen crew in your efforts.

- **Visual Aid.** One of the major culprits in high food costs is waste. Put a new garbage can in the kitchen. This can is for wasted product only, such as wrong orders, dropped food, etc. By giving your kitchen staff this visual aid, you can reinforce the amount of money that gets spent on such product waste. This will help keep your staff tuned in to keeping an eye on kitchen waste.

- **Pick a month to have the entire staff work to lower food cost**. If you're running a 38-percent food cost, tell your employees you want to try to lower it to 36 percent that month. Give them an incentive – throw a party at the end of the month if the goal is achieved. Create T-shirts and prizes to give away at the party. For example, offer a prize for the server who sold the most desserts that month or the cook who came up with the best new cost-saving measure. Not only will you cut your costs, you'll build employee morale and loyalty at the same time.

- **Make sure your cooks are using scales** and measuring ingredients. Often cooks will "free-hand it" after a while, sure that they can eyeball the correct proportions. Set up a scale. After the cook prepares an item the usual way, have the same cook prepare the item using a scale and/or measuring devices. Show the staff the difference in ingredient amounts.

Kitchen Space

The control process allows managers to establish standards and standard procedures. It is used to train all employees to follow those standards and procedures, monitor performance and take appropriate action to correct any deviations from the established procedures. Kitchen organization is a major consideration when setting up operational controls and standards.

- **Review the available facilities.** Before you create or redesign a menu, you should take a good look at your kitchen and analyze exactly what it can provide. Look at the following aspects:
  - What is the kitchen size?
  - How many stations are there?
  - How many kitchen employees do you have working the dinner or lunch rush?
  - How much and what types of equipment do you have?
  - How much storage room do you have?
  - Is your kitchen getting orders out in a timely manner?

- **Review your menu** to make the most of your facilities. If employees are getting in each other's way at certain work stations during rush periods, consider a serious menu overhaul. Perhaps your menu is appetizer heavy and you only have one employee at that station who also has to help the grill cook. If you want to keep all the appetizers, you may need to think about adding additional staff.

- **Extra staff during busy periods.** If, after reviewing the menu, you need to bring in extra staff, you may want to raise your appetizer prices to compensate. If you think your appetizer sales will decrease with a price increase, you may want to eliminate some of the choices. This way your appetizer cook can get things out correctly and on time. This more efficient service may even increase your appetizer sales even though there may be fewer choices.

- **Monitor current procedures.** When contemplating a menu change, first watch your kitchen as they prepare the current menu. Are there ways in which you could change an item's preparation or ingredients that would strengthen the menu? Are there ways to simplify preparation procedures in order to lower costs? All of these questions need to be considered when designing or redesigning a menu.

Kitchen Design

Poorly designed kitchens and equipment are a major complaint of busy chefs and assistants. Inefficiency breeds waste. Poor planning decreases productivity, increases wait times, contributes to employee turnover and distracts busy workers. Good kitchen design is an art and a science. An experienced consultant can help you balance space limitations, safety issues, food prep needs and budgets without sacrificing food quality, productivity and your staff's sanity!

- **Workflow.** There are several of different workflow patterns that can be used to create a balance between passive storage and active work areas. You'll need to accommodate areas for:
  - Hot and cold foods - prep and assembly.
  - Beverage – dispensing and storage.
  - Storage – food and non-food items.
  - Sanitation – ware washing and front-of-the-house cleaning equipment and supplies.
  - Receiving – off-loading space and inventory systems.

- **Break your kitchen activities into self-contained work stations.** Make sure that ingredients, tools, equipment, supplies and storage are within easy reach.

- **Create work triangles.** Triangle or diamond layouts give quick access to prep tables, sinks and cooking equipment. Straight-line layouts work best for assembly-line style prep and cooking where more than one person participates.

- **Draw out traffic maps.** Draw a map of your space to determine how to minimize unnecessary steps.

- **Strategic locations.** Locate your cooking and final prep areas closest to the dining room.

- **Consider placing your volume or batch cooking areas towards the back of the kitchen** and your to-go order needs nearest the dining room. Production that requires little tending shouldn't take up precious high-activity space.

- **Isolate dishwashing tasks.** The noises and chemical smell shouldn't mingle with your dining room ambiance.

- **Allow for ample open space.** People need to pass, carts need to be rolled, shelving needs to be moved, large buckets need to be wheeled and trays need to be lifted.

- **Coordinate placement of all equipment that requires venting** to share a single ventilation system and reduce costs. Check your local code require-ments on ventilation of heat- and moisture-producing equipment.

- **Include plenty of waste receptacles.** Divide your receptacles by type of waste if you will be implement-ing recycling programs. Check with your waste management company on local requirements for segregating glass, metal, paper, etc.

- **Design kitchens with multiple sets of IN and OUT doors.** Examples are doors that go directly from the dining area to the dish room (bypassing food prep) and doors from the bar to the dish room, ice machine and/or barware and liquor storage.

- **Ask your staff.** Take advantage of their daily experiences and enhance their work areas during a kitchen renovation.

Cooking Procedure Tips

The manner in which food items are cooked can have a significant effect on food yields.

- **Adhere to the proper temperatures;** high temperatures increase shrinkage and reduce yield.

- **Use accurate thermometers** and calibrate them weekly.

- **Grades of meat will have different levels of shrinkage** due to fat percentages.

- **Use convection ovens whenever possible;** they decrease cooking time and, thus, shrinkage.

- **Cooking in small batches provides the best quality** and food turnover.

- **Pot-scrubbing machine.** Continuous pot-scrubbing machines reduce the time spent on scrubbing. Power-soaking equipment will virtually eliminate the time and hassle spent scrubbing burnt or baked-on food. See www.natconcorp.com. The NC-880-GWP cleans food service pots and pans with a combination of high-power water flow and specially designed granules. A single cycle will wash and sanitize all types of cookware and serving pans in less than 5 minutes, without pre-soaking or scrubbing!

- **Storage boxes.** Cambro's storage boxes, www.cambro.com, feature a sliding lid. No need to move the box; just slide the lid back and remove what you need. Save time and strain on employees' backs. Staff also doesn't have to worry about finding a clean place to lay the lid while they get what they need from the box.

- **See-through lids.** Cambro's see-through lids for steam-table pans are another innovation you may want to consider. Labor is saved by simply snapping on a lid instead of covering and wrapping pans. More time is saved because you don't have to unwrap the pan to see what is inside. The lids fit tightly, preventing food from spilling or slopping out of the pan and less cleanup is required.

- **Coffee.** Bunn-O-Matic uses technology to ensure that your coffee will always be brewed to specifications. The machine itself makes sure that the grounds-to-water ratio is perfect every time. Future innovations will let the machine analyze and adjust the coffee as it is being brewed. For more information, visit www.bunnomatic.com.

- **PanSaver.** PanSaver is an interesting concept for food service operations. PanSaver® is a high-temperature-resistant (400° F/204° C) material which has been specifically designed to fit the standard-size pots and pans used in commercial kitchens. Simply line your pans with PanSaver and cook as usual. At the end of the night, toss the liner, or use it to store leftovers. No pan scrubbing, soaking or scouring needed. No problems with fat-laden waste going down your drains to cause clogs or hassles with your local municipalities. Straight into the trash and you are ready to start fresh the next day. Food doesn't dry out or burn as easily since it isn't in direct contact with the hot metal of the pan, resulting in less food waste. PanSaver has a line of oven bags for baking, boiling, steaming and freezing. Another line of containers is used for cook/chill, where you can prepare food ahead of time and chill it in these special containers that seal the food from contamination and dissipate heat more quickly than conventional methods. Visit Atlantic Publishing's Web site at www.atlantic-pub.com to order.

Keep in mind the following safe cooking tips as well:

- **Stir.** Stir foods cooked in deep pots frequently to ensure thorough cooking.

- **Deep frying.** When deep frying potentially hazardous foods, make sure fryers are not overloaded, and make sure the oil temperature returns to the required level before adding the next batch. Use a hot-oil thermometer designed for this special application.

- **Remember.** It's important to remember, however, that conventional cooking procedures cannot destroy bacterial spores nor deactivate their toxins.

- **Cook/chill systems.** Use the modern cook/chill systems for advance food preparation and portioning. The cook/chill system is a manufacturing process. Food is cooked to a "just done" status then immediately chilled (not frozen) for storage and reheating. The basic cook/chill concept is based on the fact that foods are cooked to the proper tempera-tures, killing most organisms and microbes, then the food is stored as close to the freezing point as possible without allowing it to actually freeze. These systems also may permit "centralized" or a central commissary, for regional food service preparation. These systems are very popular in school, prison, and cafeteria food service environments, but they lend themselves well to a traditional restaurant situation. For more information, visit the following Web sites:

- oge.apogee.net/cce/cac.htm
- www.groen.com:9097
- www.nafem.org
- www.useco.com/html/flowchart.html

- **Cook/freeze systems.** Cook/freeze systems follow the same principals as cook/chill, but rather than being rapidly chilled, the food is rapidly frozen to -20° C. This allows storage of the food for a number of months rather than 5 days, as in the cook/chill system.

Thermometers and Cooking Temperatures

The following chart shows the minimum cooking temperatures for various food items:

MINIMUM COOKING TEMPERATURES

Poultry (chicken, turkey, etc.), stuffed meats, stuffing containing meat	165° F
Ground beef (hamburger), ground fish (fish cakes)	155° F
Pork and pork products	145° F
Eggs, fish and other foods	145° F

Follow label directions for cooking commercially prepared foods. Reheat all leftovers thoroughly to 165° F or above.

Microwave cooking directions: Rotate or stir midway through cooking. Let stand covered for an additional 2 minutes. Heat to at least 165° F in all parts. If in doubt, cook all foods thoroughly to 165° F.

Calibrating a Thermometer

Using a food thermometer is the only reliable way to ensure safety and determine the "doneness" of meat, poultry and egg products. To be safe, these foods must be cooked to an internal temperature high enough to destroy any harmful microorganisms that may be in the food. "Doneness" also refers to food cooked to a desired state, including the desired texture, appearance and juiciness. Unlike the temperatures required for safety, these sensory aspects are subjective. There are two ways to check the accuracy of a food thermometer. One method uses ice water, the other uses boiling water. Many food thermometers have a calibration nut under the dial that can be adjusted. Check the package for instructions.

- **Ice water.** To use the ice-water method, fill a large glass with finely crushed ice. Add clean tap water to the top of the ice and stir well. Immerse the food thermometer stem a minimum of 2 inches into the mixture, touching neither the sides nor the bottom of the glass. Wait a minimum of 30 seconds before adjusting. (For ease in handling, the stem of the food thermometer can be placed through the clip section of the stem sheath and, holding the sheath horizontally, lowered into the water.) Without removing the stem from the ice, hold the adjusting nut under the head of the thermometer with a suitable tool and turn the head so the pointer reads 32° F.

- **Boiling water.** To use the boiling-water method, bring a pot of clean tap water to a full rolling boil. Immerse the stem of a food thermometer in boiling water a minimum of 2 inches and wait at least 30 seconds. (For ease in handling, the stem of the food thermometer can be placed through the clip section of the stem sheath and, holding the sheath horizontally, lowered into the boiling water.) Without removing the stem from the pan, hold the adjusting nut under the head of the food thermometer with a suitable tool and turn the head so the thermometer reads 212° F.

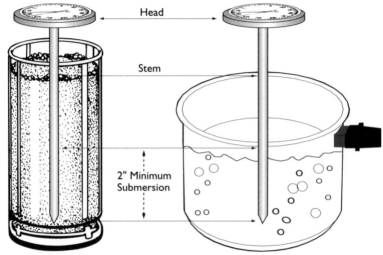

ICE WATER METHOD   **BOILING WATER METHOD**

- **Accuracy.** For true accuracy, distilled water must be used and the atmospheric pressure must be one atmosphere (29.921 inches of mercury). A consumer using tap water in unknown atmospheric conditions would probably not measure water boiling at 212° F. Most likely it would boil at least 2° F, and perhaps as much as 5° F, lower. Remember that water boils at a lower temperature in a high-altitude area. Check with the local cooperative extension service or health department for the exact temperature of boiling water in your area.

- **Inaccuracies.** Even if the food thermometer cannot be calibrated, it should still be checked for accuracy using either method. Any inaccuracies can be taken into consideration when using the food thermometer or the food thermometer can be replaced. For example, water boils at 212° F. If the food thermometer reads 214° F in boiling water, it is reading 2 degrees too high. Therefore, 2 degrees must be subtracted from the temperature displayed when taking a reading in food to find out the true temperature. For safety, ground beef patties must reach 160° F. If the thermometer is reading 2 degrees too high, 2 degrees would be added to the desired temperature, meaning hamburger patties must be cooked to 162° F.

Preparation for Service

There are several actions you and your kitchen staff can take when preparing for service that will help control costs.

- **Uniform portions.** Regulate the size and thickness of each portion to make cooking time predictable and uniform.

- **Allow cooking equipment to heat up** between batches.

- **Monitor the accuracy of heating equipment** with each use by using thermometers. In addition, always use a thermometer to ensure food reaches the proper temperature during cooking. Use a sanitized metal-stemmed, numerically scaled thermometer (accurate to plus or minus 2° F) or a digital thermometer. Check food temperature in several places, especially in the thickest parts, to make sure the food is thoroughly cooked. To avoid getting a false reading, be careful not to touch the pan or bone with the thermometer.

- **Roughly prepared ingredients are finished prior to plating.** The quality and care with which this is done determines the amount of waste generated in preparation of standard recipes.

Portioning

Pre-portioning is a very simple way to make sure that portions are always standard. Pre-portioning can be done during slow periods, saving time when the rush is on.

- **Measure everything.** Everything must be measured and portioned; this includes not only entrée portions but side dishes, sauces, condiments, garnishes, salads, salad dressings, etc. Most items will be pro-portioned in the preparation process. Many items will be weighed, but liquids will be measured using specified ladles, spoons and cups. Items such as eggs and baked potatoes should be counted.

- **Consistency.** In addition to a crucial element of cost control, accurate portioning ensures food consistency. Have you ever been in a restaurant when a waiter brings to another table the prime rib hanging off the plate, only to later receive your average-size order?

- **Quality.** Final food preparation procedures must be studied constantly to ensure quality and quantity standards. Portion-controlling all food items is an effective way to control food costs, but it also maintains consistency in the final product.

- **Follow standardized recipes.** Once the precise recipe is developed, the completed menu item should look and taste exactly the same regardless of who prepared it. A dinner presented to a customer on Tuesday must be exactly the same as it was on Saturday night.

- **Portion variance.** Portions may have a variance of up to, but not exceeding, half an ounce. Thus, if the set portion size for a steak is 12 ounces, the steak may range from 12-13 ounces. Any amount over 13 ounces must be trimmed. A light steak should be utilized for something else. Although a 1/2-ounce variance may seem like a small amount, it will actually add up very quickly. In fact, many restaurants allow a variance of only 1/8 of an ounce. If every steak with a portion size of 12 ounces is 1/2 ounce overweight, you will loose one whole steak on every 24th steak that is prepared (24 x 1/2 ounce = 12 ounces).

- **Scales.** Since portion controlling is such a vital kitchen function, purchase the best scales available. A good digital ounce scale will cost upwards of $200. However, this investment will be recouped many times over from the food-cost savings it will provide. Purchase at least two ounce-graduated scales for the kitchen and always keep a third available in reserve. One floor-type pound scale with at least a 150-pound capacity will be needed as well. This scale will be used to verify deliveries and raw yields. All scales should have a temperature-compensating device. Maintain these scales per the manufacturers' instructions; clean them periodically and oil when necessary, and they will provide years of service. To ensure the accuracy of the scales, test them periodically with an item of known weight. Most good scales come with a calibration kit. New digital scales have automatic counting functions and many are hand-free operated.

- **Portion-control bags.** Use portion-control bags and day-dated bags to control food items prior to use. These bags are ideal for all foods but can be particularly effective for items that are hard to bundle and store. For example, a side order for sautéed mushrooms can be portioned into 6-ounce portions, or an 8-ounce scallop entrée can be bagged and stored; these items can be portioned and stored in the bag ahead of cooking time, dated and rotated properly, ensuring perfect control. Contact Daymark Food Safety Systems at 800-847-0101 or www.dissolveaway.com for more information.

- **Scales must be checked weekly.** Visit the Scale Buyers' Guide, a great source for all scale manufacturers' calibration systems. Locate calibration system manufacturers and calibration system distributors at www.scalebuyersguide.com.

- **Get your employees involved.** Explain to the staff, for example, how wasting 1 ounce of shrimp on each dinner portion translates into a tremendous loss of money. If 1 ounce of shrimp costs .60 cents: .60 cents/ounce x 50 dinners a day = $30 a day x 365 days = $10,950 per year.

- **Pre-portioned items.** Purchase as many items as possible from your vendors pre-portioned. Virtually all meat, chicken, pork, fish, condiments, etc., can be purchased pre-portioned. The food cost is higher but your labor cost will be lower, and costs and consistency are ensured.

- **Spatulas.** Ensure your staff uses spatulas and spoons to scrape pans, bags, etc. New high-heat spatulas can be used effectively on heated pans, pots, etc. See www.atlantic-pub.com for high-heat spatulas.

- **Plate size.** Be certain your kitchen staff uses the correct-size dish for each menu item. If they are serving a salad on a dinner plate, they will probably serve too much, since the prescribed portion will look small on the dinner plate, and they will tend to add more food to compensate.

- **Train your staff.** Have standardized recipes charts and measuring equipment available. Charts should be laminated and posted on all kitchen walls.

To Compute Yield Percentages

To properly portion menu items, you will need to learn about yield percentages and yield tests.

ITEM	STARTING WEIGHT (OZ.)	# OF PORTIONS	TOTAL PORTION WEIGHT (OZ.)	YIELD %	PREP. COOK
Shrimp dinner	80.0	9	9 x 8.0oz = 72 oz.	90%	Bob S.

1. Compute the total amount of ounces used. Verify the amount in this column against a Sign-out Sheet. This figure is the starting weight in ounces.

2. The Amount Prepared column contains the number of portions yielded. Enter this figure on a Yield Sheet.

3. To compute the yield percentage, divide the Total Portion Weight (in ounces) by the Starting Weight (in ounces).

Yields should be consistent regardless of who prepares the item. If there is a substantial variance in the yield percentages (4-10 percent) consider these questions:

- **Are the preparation cooks carefully portioning all products?** Over the months have they gotten lax in these methods?

- **Are you purchasing the same brands of the product?** Different brands may have different yields!

- **Are all the items signed out on the Sign-out Sheet actually being used** in preparing the menu items? Is it possible some of the product is being stolen after it is issued and before it is prepared? Do certain employees preparing the food items have consistently lower yields than others?

- **Is the staff properly trained in cutting, trimming and butchering** the raw products? Do they know all the points of eliminating waste?

- **Periodically compare the average yield percentage to the percentage used in projecting the menu costs.** If the average yield has dropped, you may need to review the menu prices.

Yield Tests

A yield test is used to determine the amount of a product that is edible and the amount that is waste. Inventory yield tests should be carried out on a regular basis, especially on items that have a high perishability rate. Don't waste money on items that yield little edible product! Consider the following:

- **Quality.** Higher-quality items will usually provide more edible product. So, it's really important to be able to recognize high-quality products. Factors to look out for when deciding on product quality include:
  - Weight
  - Grade
  - Packaging
  - Color
  - Texture
  - Odor
  - Temperature
  - Size

- **Two types of yield tests.** There are two yield tests: a convenience yield test and a fresh-food yield test.

Convenience yield tests are conducted on prepackaged products and generally consist of taking the item out of its packaging and weighing it. Fresh-food yield tests are more complicated and should involve the following steps:

1. Weigh the product when it is received and again when it comes out of storage.
2. Trim excess fat, bones, etc., and weigh.
3. Wash and weigh the item again.
4. Prepare the food and weigh again to determine the amount of weight lost during the cooking process.
5. Cut the item into portion sizes.
6. Weigh the portions.

- **Record each stage of the yield test.** This information will help you decide whether or not you are wasting money on product that contains high amounts of wastage.

Presentation

Plate presentation is an important element of any menu item. Food that is presented well is perceived to have more value by the customer and your prices for well-plated food can be on the higher side of the price continuum. Three elements compose plate presentation: dish type and size, portion size and garnish. Consider the following:

- **Provide the appropriate plate sizes for menu items.** Otherwise, kitchen staff may be prone to over-portioning. For example, if a salad that should be plated on a salad dish is put on a dinner plate, the pantry person is likely to add more salad so that the item is not swallowed up by the dish. Include plate-size information on your standardized recipe.

- **Portion size should also be included on your standardized recipe.** Consistent portioning is important to customer satisfaction, especially for your regulars. Your customers may order the same dish many times. It's important that each time it comes out of the kitchen, it looks and tastes the same. Since most restaurants have various people working in the kitchen, you must put controls in place so that everyone creates the same dish the same way.

- **Garnish is often overlooked** in recipes and in presentation. For minimal cost, garnish can add to the appearance of your plates. Garnish can be anything from simple chopped parsley to sauces drizzled across the plate in a decorative manner. It's the slice of lemon on top of your salmon or the cheese croutons in the soup.

Plate Arrangement

Along with the actual garnish ingredients, think about how you want the food to be arranged on the plate. Factors to consider when arranging a plate are:

- **Layout.** Think about where you want the customer to focus. Usually a plate consists of a meat, a starch and a vegetable. Most times you want the customer to focus on the most expensive item on the plate (this will enhance the perceived value of the meal). The main element of the plate is usually the meat, so you would usually want your customer to focus on that item.

- **Balance.** Take the balance of the plate into consideration. Balance refers to the weight of the items on the plate.

- **Line.** Line is also important because a strong line has strong eye appeal. A strong line helps to draw the customer's eye to the plate.

- **Dimension/height.** Dimension or height also adds to a plate's appeal. Use molds to mound potatoes or rice and lean meat up against these mounds to create height and a three-dimensional plate. Don't overdo the height factor, however. You do not want to overwhelm the taste of the food itself by the presentation. Do not over-stack or over-portion a plate.

- **Color.** This is important in plate presentation; try to get maximum eye appeal. Perhaps top your salmon with some red pepper curls or chopped chives.

- **Maneuverability.** Keep in mind that the customer is eventually going to eat the masterpiece that you have just created. Don't make it difficult to reach around garnishes or to cut into the food.

- **Overall appearance.** Rather than just putting the sliced roast pork beside the mashed potatoes and the green beans, tie the pieces together. Place the mound of potatoes in the center of the plate and fan the slices of pork around it leaning against the mound. Tie the green beans into a bundle with a steamed chive and angle them on the other side of the potatoes. Think of the plate as a canvas and see what you can create.

- **Serviceability.** Balance durability with aesthetics.

Guest Tickets and the Cashier

There are various methods of controlling cash and guest tickets. The following will describe an airtight system of checks and balances for controlling cash, tickets and prepared food. Certain modifications may be needed to implement these controls in your own restaurant. Many of the cash registers and POS systems available on the market can eliminate most of the manual work and calculations. With a POS system, the order is entered into the system as it is received from waitstaff. With a manual system, the sale isn't recorded until the customer pays. In addition, with a POS system, the check can't be lost. The systems described in this section are based on the simplest and least expensive cash registers available.

- **Write it down.** All food or bar items must be written down in ink before the cook or bartender prepares them.

- **Guest checks.** Guest checks, when properly accounted for, will provide an audit trail to food and sales.

- **Register keys.** The register must have three separate subtotal keys for food, liquor and wine sales and a grand total key for the total guest check. Sales tax is then computed on this amount. The register also must calculate the food, liquor and wine totals for the shift. These are basic functions that most machines have.

- **Guest tickets must be of the type that is divided into two parts.** The first section is the heavy paper part listing the menu items. At the bottom is a space for the subtotals, grand total, tax and a tear-away customer receipt. The second section is a carbon copy of the first. The carbon copy is given to the expediter, who then issues it to the cooks so they can start the cooking process. Some restaurants utilize handheld ordering computers and/or the tickets may be printed in the kitchen at the time of entry into the POS system or register. Regardless, the expediter must receive a ticket in order to issue any food.

- **Guest check numbers.** The tickets must have individual identification numbers printed in sequence on both parts and the tear-away receipt. They must also have a space for the waitperson's name, date, table number and the number of people at the table. This information will be used by the expediter and bookkeeper in tracking down lost tickets and/or food items.

- **Issuing checks.** Each member of the waitstaff is issued a certain number of tickets each shift. These tickets are in numbered sequence. For example, a waitperson may be issued 25 tickets from 007575 to 007600. At the end of the shift, he or she must return to the cashier the same total number of tickets. No ticket should ever become lost; it is the responsibility of the waitstaff to ensure this.

WAITPERSON	TOT #	#THRU	INITIALS	RETURN # VERIFIED

- **Mistakes.** Should there be a mistake on a ticket, the cashier must void out all parts. This ticket must be turned in with the others after being approved and signed by the manager.

- **Giveaways.** In certain instances, the manager may approve of giving away menu items at no charge. The manager must also approve of the discarding of food that cannot be served. A ticket must be written to record all of these transactions. To follow are some examples of these types of situations:

- **Manager food.** All food that is issued free of charge to managers, owners and officers of the company.

- **Complimentary food.** All food issued to a customer compliments of the restaurant. This includes all food given away as part of a promotional campaign.

- **Housed food.** All food which is not servable, such as spoiled, burned or incorrect orders.

- **Cashier report form.** All of these tickets should be filled out as usual, listing the items and the prices. The cashier should not ring up these tickets, but record them on the Cashier Report Form (see example on the following page). Write the word "manager," "complimentary" or "housed" over the top of the ticket.

- **Cash drawer.** The manager issues a cash drawer, or "bank," to the cashier. The drawers are prepared by the bookkeeper. Inside the cashier drawer is the Cashier Report itemizing the breakdown of the money it contains.

- **Accuracy of Cashier Report.** The accuracy of the Cashier Report is the responsibility of both the cashier and the manager. Upon receiving the cash drawer, the cashier must count the money in the cash drawer with the manager to verify its contents. After verification, the cashier will be responsible for the cash register. The cashier should be the only employee allowed to operate it.

- **Each member of the waitstaff will bring his or her guest ticket to the cashier for totaling.** The cashier must examine the ticket to ensure:
  - All items were charged for.
  - All items have the correct price.

- All bar and wine tabs are included.
- Subtotals and grand total are correct.
- Sales tax is entered correctly.

CASHIER REPORT FORM

Prepared By: _____

Date: _____ Day: _____ Shift: _____

		BAR REGISTER		SERVICE REGISTER		TOTAL
		Day	Night	Day	Night	All Shifts
1	BANK DEPOSIT Part I					
2	Currency					
3	Silver					
4	Checks					
5	SUB TOTAL					
6	CREDIT CARDS:					
7	MasterCard/Visa					
8	American Express					
9	Diners Club					
10	Other					
11	OTHER RECEIPTS:					
12	TOTAL BANK DEPOSIT					
13	CASH SUMMARY Part II					
14	Sales per Register					
15	Sales Tax per Register					
16	ADJUSTMENTS:					
17	Over/Under Rings					
18	Other: Complimentaries					
19	Other					
20	TOTAL ADJUSTMENTS					
21	Sales to Be Accounted For					
22	Sales Tax to Be Acctd. For					
23	Accounts Collected					
24	Other Receipts:					
25						
26						
27	TIPS CHARGED:					
28	MasterCard/Visa					
29	American Express					
30	Diners Club					
31	Other					
32	House Accounts-Tips					
33	TOTAL RECEIPTS					
34	DEDUCT: PAID OUTS					
35	Tips Paid Out					
36	House Charges					
37	Total Deductions					
38	NET CASH RECEIPTS					
39	BANK DEPOSIT (Line 12)					
40	OVER or SHORT					

- **Charge card forms.** The cashier is responsible for filling out the charge card forms and ensuring their accuracy. The cashier will return the customer's charge card and receipt to the appropriate member of the waitstaff.

- **Cashing out.** At the end of each shift, the cashier must cash out with the manager. List all the cash in the "Cash Out" columns. Enter the breakdown of sales into separate categories. Do not include sales tax. Enter all complimentary, housed and manager amounts. Itemize all checks on the back. Itemize each ticket for total sales and total dinner count. Break down and enter all charged sales.

- **The total amount of cash taken in plus the charge sales must equal the total itemized ticket sales.** Itemize all checks on the back of the Cashier Report and stamp "FOR DEPOSIT ONLY." The stamp should include the restaurant's bank name and account number.

- **Charged tips.** Should a customer charge a tip, you may give the waiter or waitress a "cash paid out" from the register. When the payment comes in, you can then deposit the whole amount into your account. Miscellaneous paid-outs are for any items that may need to be purchased throughout the shift. List all of them on the back and staple the receipts to the page.

- **When everything is checked out and balanced, the sheet must be signed by the cashier and manager.** The manager should then deposit all tickets, register tapes, cash, charges and forms into the safe for the bookkeeper the next morning. The cash on hand must equal the register receipt readings. The bookkeeper will perform an audit and prepare the bank deposit.

- **POS training.** Ensure all employees are trained on the computer POS system. Poor training will result in incorrect orders, add-ons not being charged for and cooking instructions being neglected. Many systems allow a ticket to be voided instead of housed or comped, which means you will lose a credit in the monthly food-cost calculation.

CHAPTER EIGHT

SECURITY & SAFETY

Restaurant Security

Keeping your restaurant secure and safe can go a long way in helping you control and reduce food costs.

- **Have your back door hooked up to a small buzzer** so that anytime it's opened, a small noise sounds letting anyone in the kitchen and office know. Using this feature will also keep customers, inspectors and even the competition from sneaking a peek into your kitchen. Since a wide-open door invites bugs, rodents and outside noise into your kitchen, this not only provides security but an incentive to keep your kitchen environment safely contained.

- **Utilize an employee login for your POS system** wherever possible. Make sure employees know that these numbers are for their own good and that sharing their numbers puts their safety in jeopardy. Systems like this not only let you keep track of who is opening a register, but which employees are busiest, fastest and make the least number of mistakes.

- **Install alarms.** Installing alarms on exit doors marked for "emergency use only" will keep your clientele and employees from walking out when they're not supposed to, as well as keeping outsiders from sneaking into areas they're not supposed to be in. For more information on door chimes and alarms, take a look at these online alarm retailers: Chime

City at www.chimecity.com or Drive Alert at
www.drivealert.com.

- **Security cameras.** Consider installing security
  cameras or, at the very least, "fake" cameras at exit
  doors and cash areas. This will keep your staff on
  their toes and your customers from getting sneaky.

- **Mistakes.** Have your employees place any "mistakes"
  on a shelf for management review and document as
  to why and how the mistake occurred. Using, and
  sticking to, this method will make certain that
  employees and managers take spoilage and waste
  seriously. It also will deter theft.

Guest Check and Cash Drawer Security

Never make an outgoing check to cash, and don't accept
them either. With a "cash" check, anyone could deposit
the check as his or her own, or worse: the receiver of the
check could bank it and claim it never arrived. Your check
is always your last chance for a receipt, and security of
that check is paramount.

- **Keep all unused checks locked in a safe.** Keeping
  tabs on all check number successions and taking
  action if checks are missing will help you keep tabs
  on your money. You always have the option of
  stopping payment if need be, but if you don't spot a
  problem quickly, you may never get that chance.

- **Limit all access to petty cash.** Petty cash is the
  numbe-one area of office fraud, and if yours isn't
  under lock and key, you can almost guarantee it'll
  find its way out the door.

- **The person who signs your company checks should also be the person who mails them.** This ensures your checks find their way to the company they're intended for and makes certain you don't pay any "fake" invoices.

- **Use a second.** The manager responsible for writing deposit slips, counting money and marking the deposit entry in your books should always be seconded by another person, especially when it's being deposited, to ensure that nothing goes amiss between the office and the bank.

- **Customer checks.** Bad checks are a major source of customer theft. Try to avoid accepting checks unless you know the customer well, and if you absolutely must take a check, be sure to check the ID of the person signing it.

- **Credit cards.** When accepting credit cards, always have your employees check the signature on the card against the signature on the receipt. To ensure they do this, have them write "verified" on the receipt after they do so.

- **Customer changes.** Occasionally, a customer will claim to have been given change for a smaller bill than they originally handed over. In this situation, if it's possible to "Z" the register and run a quick cash count to verify the cash drawer contents, then do so. If you're too busy to close out a register, get the customer's name and phone number and tell them you will call them as soon as the drawer has been balanced. Forward any overage to them at your own cost. Certainly, you don't want to lose a customer if you can help it, but being an easy target for fraud can do even more damage to your bottom line.

- **Remove cash from the register throughout the night.** At various times throughout the night, under the supervision of the cashier involved, have your manager "bundle" any notes that number 12 or more in the cash drawer into bundles of 10, and then move them to the safe, replacing them in the drawer with signed requisition slips. This keeps the end-of-the-night count simple, and it keeps large amounts of cash out of the place where it's most vulnerable.

- **Return promptly with bill.** In order to prevent customer walkouts, after presenting the bill, the server should return to the table promptly for payment, or at the very least, keep a constant eye on the customers.

- **Position of cashier.** Having your cashier located at the only non-alarmed exit door will not prevent customers from leaving without paying, but it will certainly make such a move more risky for them. If your hosting employees are alert and attentive, your customer walkouts should be cut to a minimum.

Bank Deposits/Accounts Payable

Proper auditing of bank deposits and charges slips must be conducted to ensure all deposits were made and to account for missing checks. Upon receipt of the bank statement, don't put it aside for your accountant; reconcile it yourself and you will gain new insight into the business and close the last loophole where money could escape. Use the form on the back of your bank statement or use your computer software program and follow this step-by-step method.

1. Check addition and subtraction in your checkbook through the end of the month.

2. Compare each canceled check with your cash disbursements journal to be sure the amounts agree. Check them off as you go.

3. Mark the check stub for each check you have received.

4. Mark each amount on the bank statement to indicate you have compared the check.

5. Compare deposit slips with your checkbook.

6. If you have deposit slips for deposits not marked in your checkbook, add the amount at the end of the month with the date of the deposit.

7. Mark your checkbook and/or cash receipts journal for each deposit slip you have received.

8. Mark each deposit slip to indicate you have compared it.

9. Mark each deposit amount on the bank statement to indicate you have compared the deposit.

10. Record any bank notices or charges (e.g., new checks, returned checks, etc.) in the checkbook and cash disbursements journal at the end of the month.

11. If a check you deposited was returned:

    a. subtract the amount from your balance at the end of the month;

    b. note on the deposit and on the end-of-the-month statement why you are subtracting this amount, who the check was from, and why it was returned;

    c. make a copy of the check and return notice to keep with your records; and

    d. send the original check back to your bank for recollection efforts.

12. Voided checks. If you have voided a check, keep the defaced original with your check stub and cross out the amount in your checkbook and disbursements journal so that it is not treated as a check amount.

Kitchen-Safety Procedures

Ensuring your patrons and staff aren't injured on the premises is more than a matter of caring for their well being; it's an essential part of avoiding a business-threatening lawsuit and lengthy downtime. Labor and food savings, insurance savings, workers' compensation reductions and sick pay savings, not to mention staying out of civil court, all come from putting safety procedures in place and sticking to them.

- **Equipment.** Make sure that equipment, tools, machinery and substances are in safe working condition.

- **Employees.** Talk to your workers about safety in the workplace and encourage open discussion.

- **Facilities.** Maintain safe and hygienic facilities including toilets and eating areas.

- **Information.** Offer information, training and supervision for all workers.

- **Procedures.** Implement processes to inform workers and involve them in decisions that may affect their health and safety at work. Implement processes for identifying hazards, assessing risks and controlling risks.

- **Injuries.** Record work-related injuries and illnesses.

- **Awareness.** Pay attention to safe work. Your business will not only become more competitive, but you can help stop the pain and suffering from workplace injury or fatality.

- **Use safety signs.** Safety signs are usually available for free from your local Department of Health or Labor or your appliance manufacturers. Keep these posted around your kitchen. Signs will include details on how to lift heavy items safely, directions on proper signage for slippery floors and dangerous equipment, and rules on who handles jobs like lighting gas pilots, changing light bulbs and sharpening knives. Some signs can be downloaded from www.restaurantbeast.com.

Basic Knife Safety

These basic knife-safety tips will help prevent injuries and accidents. Be aware of the following:

- **Keep your knives sharp.**

- **Don't cut with the edge toward you** or your fingers.

- **Don't leave sharp knives loose in a drawer.**

- **Let it fall.** If you are working with or handling a knife and you drop it, stand back and let it fall; don't try to catch it.

- **Dishwasher.** If you have a dirty knife, don't toss it in the dishwater. You don't want the dishwasher to come up with a handful of sharp knifes.

- **Edge.** Don't lay it down with the edge pointing up.

- **Videos and books are available on knife handling** and safety at www.atlantic-pub.com.

Other Safety Tips

- **Blade-resistant gloves.** Ask a kitchen staff volunteer to tape the thumb on his hands to his palm. Then ask him to tie his shoes, open a door, drink a soda, slice a tomato and drive a car. All employees will soon realize the importance of wearing cut-resistant gloves. A study by the National Safety Council states hand lacerations cost employers an average of $3,337 in expenses and lost productivity. Gloves cost about $15 per hand. Knit cut-resistant gloves give greater levels of dexterity and comfort; they are made with fabric reinforced with a combination of strong fibers including stainless steel. Metal mesh gloves, made of double-interlocked welded rings (think of a suit of armor), are used by butchers, meat processors, chefs and ice carvers. They provide the highest level of cut resistance. Gloves are available at www.atlantic-pub.com.

- **Burns.** Steam, oil and grease, boiling soups, hot grills and ovens, can all result in workplace burn injuries. The Burn Foundation has found that such injuries tend to occur when managers don't enforce safety rules or when workers themselves are careless about safety. The potential for accidents is also greater when workers are worn out, on drugs or alcohol or are simply taking unnecessary risks. Every restaurant is fast-paced with congested areas; these are the ingredients needed for a disaster.

- **Shortening Shuttles.** Transporting hot waste oil from the fryer is very dangerous. Very serious accidents have occurred as the night crew changes the oil at the end of the shift. They are tired and want to go home and may be rushing. Consider purchasing Shortening Shuttles®. These inexpensive devices make hot-oil transfer safe and easy and virtually eliminate the dangers and liability of exposure to hot-oil burns. For more information on these devices, visit www.shortening-shuttle.com or call 800-533-5711.

- **Protection.** Wear protective gloves or mitts when handling hot pots or cooking with hot, deep-frying oil.

- **Shoes**. Wear non-skid shoes to prevent slipping on wet or greasy tile floors.

- **Grease fires.** Extinguish hot oil/grease fires by sliding a lid over the top of the container.

- **Hot oil.** Never carry or move oil containers when the oil is hot or on fire.

- **Reaching.** Avoid reaching over or across hot surfaces and burners; use barriers, guards or enclosures to prevent contact with hot surfaces.

- **Directions.** Read and follow directions for proper use of electrical appliances.

- **First aid.** Keep first-aid kits readily available. Make sure at least one person on each shift has first-aid training.

- **Keep fire extinguishers accessible** and up to date.

- **Safety course.** The National Restaurant Association's Educational Foundation offers an educational program called AWARE: Employee &

Customer Safety. The nine modules offered include sections on ensuring fire safety in the kitchen and preventing burns. The Educational Foundation also offers videos with an interactive CD-ROM that promote workplace safety and focus on how to prevent on-the-job injuries.

- **Mopping.** Ensure anyone mopping a floor area puts out ample signage to indicate the floor is wet and may be slippery. This doesn't mean a single yellow cone; it means enough signage so that a person has to actually make an effort just to get to the slippery floor.

- **Coolers and storage.** Keep any heavy coolers or storage fridges located at or above waist level wherever possible.

- **Keep your food supply safe.** Make sure your employees are trained in food service sanitation. Check with area community colleges for courses in food safety and sanitation. The National Restaurant Association also offers ServSafe, certification courses through Atlantic Publishing at www.atlantic-pub.com.

- **HACCP (Hazard Analysis Critical Control Point).** Have a HACCP system in place. HACCP was developed by NASA about 30 years ago to keep astronauts' food supply safe. Until recently, HACCP was almost exclusively used in food production plants, but restaurants are beginning to adopt this approach to food safety. Having a HACCP system in place could save you a fortune in liability costs. If a situation arises, you may be able to prove you were using reasonable care and this can go a long way in a liability suit. There are seven basic principals HACCP uses. Basically, these principals indicate that you need to identify all the critical points at which food can become unsafe, such as during cooking, storage and production. Then you must put measures in place to ensure food remains safe. These measures can include actions such as establishing minimum cooking times for menu items and having policies about how long food can remain at room temperature before it must be thrown away. Additionally, you must establish methods to monitor that these policies are being followed and you must establish corrective actions to take if the safety measures have not been used. For more information on HACCP, HACCP checklists and HACCP form templates, log on to the Food Safety, Education and Training Alliance's Web site at www.fstea.org/resources/tooltime/forms.html.

The High Cost of Food-Borne Illness

Food-borne illnesses cost lives and money. According to the FDA, millions of people become sick each year and thousands die after eating contaminated or mishandled foods. Children, the elderly and people with weakened immune systems are especially vulnerable to food-borne illness.

- **Costly.** The National Restaurant Association estimates the average cost of a food-borne illness outbreak at more than $75,000.

- **Serving safe food has numerous benefits.** By preventing food-borne illness outbreaks, establish-ments can avoid legal fees, medical claims, wasted food, bad publicity and closure of the establishment.

What Makes Food Unsafe?

Hazards can be introduced into foodservice operations in numerous ways: by employees, food, equipment, cleaning supplies and customers. The hazards may be biological (including bacteria and other microorganisms), chemical (including cleaning agents) or physical (including glass chips and metal shavings).

- **Microbiological hazards.** Microbiological hazards (bacteria in particular) are considered the greatest risk to the food industry. Bacteria usually require food, acidity, temperature, time, oxygen and moisture in order to grow. Controlling any or all of these factors can help prevent bacterial growth.

- **Temperature and time.** Temperature and time are the two most controllable factors for preventing food-borne illness. The temperature range between 41° F and 140° F is considered the "danger zone" because these temperatures are very conducive to bacterial growth. Within this range, bacteria grow most rapidly from 60° F to 120° F. When the conditions are right, bacteria double in number every 10-30 minutes. For instance, in three hours one bacterium can grow into thousands of bacteria. Cooking food to safe temperature and cooling food quickly, therefore, are critical steps in the prevention of food-borne illness.

Weighing the Risks

Certain foods and food service procedures are more hazardous than others. High-protein foods, such as meats and milk-based products and foods that require a lot of handling during preparation, require special attention by food service operations. Roast beef, turkey, ham and Chinese foods, for instance, have been linked with more outbreaks of food-borne illnesses than pizza, barbecued meat or egg salad, yet all of these foods are considered potentially hazardous. Other foods, such as garlic in oil, rice, melon and sprouts, also have been linked with outbreaks of food-borne illness.

Researchers at the Center for Disease Control (CDC) have identified common threads between outbreaks of food-borne illnesses. Outbreaks usually involve one or more of these factors:

- **Improper cooling of foods is** the leading cause of food-borne illness outbreaks.

- **Advance preparation of food** (with a 12-hour or more lapse before service).

- **Infected employees** with poor personal hygiene.

- **Failure to reheat cooked foods** to temperatures that kill bacteria.

- **Improper hot holding temperatures.**

- **Adding raw, contaminated ingredients to food** that receives no further cooking.

- **Foods from unsafe sources.**

- **Cross-contamination of cooked food** by raw food, improperly cleaned and sanitized equipment or employees who mishandle food.

- **Improper use of leftovers.**

- **Failure to heat or cook food thoroughly.**

Common Food-Handling Problems

The following section lists some of the most common food handling problems in restaurants:

- **Sink-side nailbrushes are missing or not used.** You can order nail and hand brush kits at www.atlantic-pub.com.

- **Failure to change protective gloves between tasks.**

- **Work tables and cutting boards not properly sanitized** between uses.

- **Food sitting out for long periods.**

- **Food such as flour and sugar stored in open containers.**

- **Deliveries left out too long before being put away.**

- **Food delivery boxes picked up from the floor** and unpacked directly on tables.

- **Equipment not cleaned.**

- **Empty soap dispensers in restrooms.**

What You and Your Staff Can Do to Prevent Food-Borne Illnesses

An important part of the production process is keeping food safe. Make sure you have HACCP procedures in place and train your kitchen staff in food safety. Here are a few simple things to do now to be sure your employees are keeping your food items safe:

- **Buy and use separate color-coded cutting boards** for all food products to prevent cross-contamination. See www.atlantic-pub.com for these products.

- **Use a sanitizer to clean surfaces** that come into contact with food.

- **Keep raw products separate** from ready-to-serve foods.

- **Sanitize cutting boards, knives and other food contact surfaces** after each contact with a potentially hazardous food.

- **Discard any leftover batter, breading or marinade** after it has been used with potentially hazardous foods.

- **Never interrupt the cooking process.** Partially cooking poultry or meat, for example, may produce conditions that encourage bacterial growth.

Hand-Washing Exercise

Make sure employees wash their hands. "Are your hands really clean?" Hand washing is perhaps the most critical aspect of good personal hygiene in food service. Workers should wash their hands with soap and warm water for 20 seconds. When working with food, they should wash gloved hands as often as bare hands. Hand washing is a simple yet effective method for eliminating cross-contamination. To illustrate the importance of hand washing to your staff, try the following exercise. First, you'll need a fluorescent substance and a black light. (One possible source for these is Atlantic Publishing's Glo Germ Training Kit. See www.atlantic-pub.com or call 800-541-1336.) Using these materials, you can show trainees the "invisible dirt" that may be hiding on their hands:

1. Have employees dip their hands in the fluorescent substance.

2. Tell employees to wash their hands.

3. Have employees hold their hands under the black light to see how much "dirt" is still there.

4. Explain proper hand-washing technique.

5. Have employees wash their hands again, this time using the proper hand-washing technique.

6. Have employees once again hold their hands under the black light.

Thawing and Marinating

- **Freezing food keeps most bacteria from multiplying, but it does not kill them**. Bacteria that are present when food is removed from the freezer may multiply rapidly if thawed at room temperature.

- **It is critical to thaw foods out of the "temperature danger zone."** NEVER thaw foods on a counter or in any other non-refrigerated area!

- **Some foods can be cooked from the frozen state**, such as frozen vegetables, pre-formed hamburger patties and chicken nuggets. It is important to note, however, that this method depends on the size of the item. For example, this method is not recommended for large foods like a 20-pound turkey.

- **The two best methods for thawing foods are:** in refrigeration at a temperature below 40° F, placed in a pan on the lowest shelf so juices cannot drip on other foods. Or, under clean, drinkable running water at a temperature of 70° F or less for no more than two hours.

- **Even when potentially hazardous foods are properly thawed, bacteria and other contaminants may still be present.** Cooking foods to the proper internal temperature will kill any existing bacteria and make food safe.

- **ALWAYS marinate meat, fish and poultry in the refrigerator.** NEVER marinate at room temperature and NEVER save and reuse marinade. As with all methods, be careful not to cross-contaminate!

Cautions for Cold Foods

When you are preparing cold foods, you are at one of the most hazardous points in the food-preparation process. There are two key reasons for this: First, cold food preparation usually takes place at room temperature. Second, cold food is one of the most common points of contamination and cross-contamination.

- **Chicken salad, tuna salad, potato salad with eggs and other protein-rich salads are common sources of food-borne illness.** Sandwiches prepared in advance and held unrefrigerated are also dangerous.

- **Preparation is key.** Because cold foods such as these receive no further cooking, it is essential that all ingredients used in them are properly cleaned, prepared and, where applicable, cooked. It is a good idea to chill meats and other ingredients and combine them while chilled.

Here are several other important precautions to keep in mind:

- Prepare foods no further in advance than necessary.

- Prepare foods in small batches and place in cold

storage immediately. This will prevent holding food too long in the "temperature danger zone."

- Always keep prepared cold foods below 40° F.

- Wash fresh fruits and vegetables with plain water to remove surface pesticide residues and other impurities, such as soil particles.

- Use a brush to scrub thick-skinned produce, if desired.

Web Site References

Some sites providing tips in the area of food service hygiene and safety include the following

The Minnesota State Department of Health
www.health.state.mn.us

MSU's Insight Into Safety
healthed.msu.edu/student/cteam.html

U.S. FDA Center for Food Safety and Applied Nutrition
vm.cfsan.fda.gov/list.html

United States Department of Agriculture's Food Safety and Inspection Service
www.usda.gov/fsis

Gateway to U.S. Government Food Safety Information
www.foodsafety.gov

Bad Bug Book
vm.cfsan.fda.gov/~mow/intro.html

Safety Alerts
www.safetyalerts.com

E. Coli Food Safety News: MedNews.Net®
www.MedNews.Net/bacteria

Safe Food Consumer
www.safefood.org

Food Safe Program
foodsafe.ucdavis.edu/homepage.html

International Food Safety Council
www.nraef.org/ifsc/ifsc_about.asp?level1_id=2&
level2_id=1

The Burn Foundation
www.burnfoundation.org

Food Irradiation

Food irradiation is a hotly debated area right now. The Food and Drug Administration has approved irradiation of meat and poultry and allows its use for a variety of other foods, including fresh fruits and vegetables and spices. The agency determined that the process is safe and effective in decreasing or eliminating harmful bacteria. Irradiation also reduces spoilage, bacteria, insects and parasites. In certain fruits and vegetables, it inhibits sprouting and delays ripening. For example, irradiated strawberries stay unspoiled up to 3 weeks versus 3-5 days for untreated berries.

- **Cost.** You should know that if you buy irradiated food, it will cost more. Industry experts estimate the increase at 2-3 cents per pound for fruits and vegetables and 3-5 cents a pound for meat and poultry products. But these costs may be offset by advantages such as keeping a product fresh longer and enhancing its safety. However, the treatment will also bring benefits to consumers in terms of availability and quantity, storage life, convenience and improved hygiene of the food. Federal rules require irradiated foods to be labeled as such to distinguish them from non-irradiated foods.

CHAPTER NINE

TECHNOLOGY

The introduction of technology to the restaurant industry cannot be understated. With profit margins reported for most restaurants in the 3-5 percent range, the introduction of technology is one of the few opportunities for cutting costs, improving efficiency and affecting the bottom line. One of the best uses of technology is, of course, the computer and POS systems, but there are others. Technology is transforming food service operations in ways that can greatly reduce dependence on human beings. Less highly skilled (and expensive) employees are needed when the equipment does the work. Pushing a button doesn't take much skill or knowledge.

Electronic Ordering Systems

In recent years many restaurants have switched to an "Electronic Guest Check System" or "Wireless Waiter." These systems use a mobile computer. The waitperson carries the mobile computer pad and places the order on the touch-screen display. As each dish is entered, this information is transferred in real time to the kitchen where the order is printed out. The drink order is taken first and sent to the bar. The mobile computer, which the waitperson carries, is then notified by a beep or vibration when the order is ready for pickup, or a "runner" delivers the meal.

- **Multiple orders.** The waitstaff can place multiple orders using a "Wireless Waiter" without ever walking into the kitchen or bar to check for previously placed orders or to pick up prepared orders. The waitstaff in the dining area of the restaurant never leaves the sight of their customers and the bill is calculated automatically, removing the risk of human error. Most systems have an optional snap-on credit card reader, which can be attached to the bottom of the handheld device. Customer credit cards are swiped through the handheld unit and processed. Under this system, customers can feel confident that their credit cards are safe, since they are never out of sight.

- **Labor savings.** Because waitstaff will always be visible in the dining area, customers will be able to easily get their waitperson's attention. In addition, servers will be able to wait on six or seven tables at a time, twice as many as before. If more tables are waited on, more tables can be turned, providing the opportunity to increase sales volume. You might need fewer waitpersons utilizing this system, since each one will be able to handle more customers. This would, of course, result in a reduction of labor costs.

POS Systems

According to information published by the National Restaurant Association, a restaurant averaging $1,000,000 in food and beverage sales can expect to see an estimated savings of $30,000 per year using a POS system. Understanding the numbers collected by a POS system will give the operator more control over inventory, bar revenues, labor scheduling, overtime, customer traffic, and service.

- **POS systems reduce the opportunities for employees to pilfer.** If your servers or other employees simply can't obtain any food without a hard-copy check or without entering the sale electronically, you have eliminated most of their opportunity to pilfer.

- **Two parts of a POS system.** A point-of-sale system comprises two parts: the hardware, or equipment, and the software, the computer program that runs the system. This system allows waitstaff to key in their orders as soon as the customers give them. Additional keys are available for particular options and specifications, such as "rare," "medium-rare," and "well-done." Some systems prompt the waitstaff to ask additional questions when the item is ordered, such as, "Would you like butter, sour cream or chives with the baked potato?" Some will suggest a side dish or a compatible wine.

- **Processing the order.** The order is sent through a cable to printers located throughout the restaurant: at the bar and in the kitchen and office. All orders must be printed before they are prepared, ensuring good control.

- **Payment.** When a server has completed the ordering, a guest check can be printed and later presented to the customer for payment. Most POS systems allow certain discounts and require manager control over others. Charge cards, cash and checks can be processed separately and then reports can be generated by payment type.

- **POS enhancements.** Many POS systems have been greatly enhanced to include the following: comprehensive home delivery, guest books, online reservations, frequent diner modules, real-time inventory, integrated caller ID, accounting, labor scheduling, payroll, menu analysis, purchasing and receiving, cash management and reports. Up-and-coming enhancements and add-ons include improved functionality across the Internet, centralized functionality enabling "alerts" to be issued to managers and voice-recognition POS technology.

POS Web Sites for Additional Information

- www.squirrelsystems.com
- www.alohaenterprise.com
- www.nextpos.com/english/overtureredirprod-ucts.htm
- www.navitech.com/cat-possystems.asp
- www.datadesignsonline.com/pos2.html
- www.microworks.com
- www.bmccomputers.com
- www.restaurant-pos.com
- www.restaurantpos.com
- www.touch2000.com/touchsystems.htm
- www.tradewindsoftware.com
- www.touchnserve.com
- www.chefsystems.com
- www.radiantsystems.com
- http://managementsolutions1.com

- **POS in the future.** As the labor market continues to diminish, touch screens with POS systems will become essential. It has been predicted that in the next few years, customers may even place their own orders. Terminals will be simply turned around. During peak seasonal periods, ordering food may be like pumping your own gas; customers will key in their own selections and then slide their credit cards through to pay.